Look
Back to
Get Ahead

Look
Back to
Get Ahead

Life Lessons from History's Heroes

MICHAEL ANTHONY
JACKSON

Arcade Publishing • New York

FIRST U.S. EDITION 2004

First published in the United Kingdom by Arrow in 2003

Library of Congress Cataloging-in-Publication Data

Jackson, Michael Anthony.
   Look back to get ahead : life lessons from history's heroes / by
Michael Anthony Jackson. —1st U.S. ed.
      p. cm.
Includes bibliographical references.
   ISBN 1-55970-727-5
   1. Success in business. 2. Entrepreneurship. 3. Success. 4. Courage—
Moral and ethical aspects. 5. Heroes—Psychological aspects.
   I. Title.

HF5386.J29 2003
650.1—dc22   2003020374

Published in the United States by Arcade Publishing, Inc., New York
Distributed by Time Warner Book Group

Visit our Web site at www.arcadepub.com

10 9 8 7 6 5 4 3 2 1

EB

PRINTED IN THE UNITED STATES OF AMERICA

Contents

Nurture your mind with great thoughts; to believe in the heroic makes heroes.

Benjamin Disraeli

The further backward you look, the further forward you can see.

Winston Churchill

Introduction: In Pursuit of Life

IN SOCIAL GATHERINGS I AM INVARIABLY INTRODUCED AS "the man who climbed K2." Then the questions start. "What was it like?" "Why did you go?" I try to satisfy them by smiling and saying, "It was cold," and changing the subject, but that never seems to work. And, invariably, three sentences of revealed horrors later, the color has drained from their faces, the conversation falters and a tense silence hangs as we stare at our drinks. I hate it. But still it does not stop them from asking . . .

So let's begin. What *was* it like?

WEEKS ONE AND TWO: WARM-UP ON NANGA PARBAT MOUNTAIN

Spent last few days on the Karokorum highway, following the Indus, crossing deserts. Many of the locals are the descendants of Alexander the Great's soldiers and Genghis Khan's horsemen. Women of exquisite beauty stand by the roadside bent double under crushing burdens, never seen children so happy and not a GameBoy in sight.

Nanga Parbat Mountain is a mirror of ice towering over the Stone Age villages. Every night there is a crowd of locals outside our tent asking for medicine. I try to do the best I can but it breaks my heart.

Found the porters gathered outside my tent this morning. They had brought a sixteen-year-old boy with them. He had been tending his flock last night, tripped and slashed his wrist open on a rock. In an attempt to stem the blood he had filled the gash with dirt! It was already turning septic. Gave him an antibiotic injection and told the porters to hold him down while I scraped the dirt out. He did not even flinch. His tendons were twanging like broken guitar strings but he just looked at me impassively like I was reading his palm. What manner of people are these? I feel so humbled by them.

I can't believe it! I told the porters to take the boy to hospital (three days' walk) but he would not go as he had to work. He tried to hide when I saw him. I checked his wound and it was gangrenous. I've just heard from our guide that it had to be amputated! Damn it; I should have taken him myself.

Sher, my guide, is coming to K2 with me.

WEEK THREE: K2 BASE CAMP

We had our first death today. A young French climber and friend of mine went to bed at base camp and died in his sleep with a cerebral edema, which happens at high altitude when fluid leaks out of blood vessels, causing the brain to swell. He was twenty years old. I'm trying to eat my breakfast but I can see his corpse lying in a body bag on the glacier. We are trying to keep him fresh. I feel sick. It'll probably be days before the helicopter arrives to carry him away to a distant land and broken-hearted parents.

The sun is setting. It's sub-zero. The porters are laying out their prayer mats and I can hear the mountains reverberate with their devotions. Belief in God seems to be an academic debate in Scotland. Life is so easy there. This place is stripping me, both physically and emotionally. I wish I could believe in something. I find myself thinking of the forgotten God of my childhood and pray that he will keep me safe in his arms as I climb, not for my sake, but so that I don't break my mother's heart.

I feel my heart clenching. My face is set in a constant grimace. The smile has been slowly dripping off my face since I came here. I can't remember the last time I laughed. Spoke to my dad on the satellite phone; wanted to tell him that I am so ashamed of the man I had been: of all the days that I squandered in apathy, complacency, the vanities, the egotism. Wanted to thank him for all the sacrifices he had made. How could I have taken it for granted and ever thought that my blessed life there was incomplete?

If this place spares me I swear I'll make a difference when I get back. I've just packed up my bag (55 pounds of it!). We start climbing at midnight. . . .

Week Four: K2

I've never known exhaustion so complete, I feel as if I ripped my soul on the ice and it bled itself dry down the mountainside. We were crossing an ice field when the climber I was roped to went through a crevasse. It felt like the world had been tipped on its side, my feet were ripped from below me and I raced backwards through the air as if I was being sucked through a wind tunnel. The ice faces and rock falls are lethal. I can still hear the screams of the French climbers today as we grasped the rock face, blocks of ice the size of giants' fists thundering past our heads. I just hung there whimpering like an abandoned child, expecting my head to be caved in at any moment. . . .

WEEK FIVE: K2

An avalanche nearly killed me today. It carried with it two dead bodies from past expeditions. One of them was broken in two. Their jagged limbs protruded from the snow like broken sailors washed ashore in a storm of ice. K2 is like a mythical beast. It does not just kill, it preserves its victims as trophies. They'll hang there for eternity or until the world thaws. People say that the dead look serene but these were twisted into grotesque parodies of men. Like Dante's Judas, frozen in the Ninth Circle of Hell.

WEEK SIX: K2

Sher collapsed three days ago with a pneumothorax (collapsed lung). They wouldn't send a helicopter because he was too poor. If he did not get to hospital he would be dead in three days. I could not let him die so I had no choice but to carry him myself and now we are both dying. I have degenerated into a dehydrated, frost-bitten wreck. I have carried him for three days and am still a day away from help. I haven't the strength to walk any further. I don't want to die here. I wanted to do so much more. I wish I had been a better man. It breaks my heart to think that all that will be left to prove I ever lived will be my family's tears. . . .

TWO DAYS LATER

God knows how but . . . we made it. Sher is in a hospital and the doctor says he will live. The doctor freaked out when I stumbled in with him on my back. I smile when I think of Sher's wife and two wee daughters. I'm heading back now.

THREE DAYS LATER

Received the greatest honor of my life today. Walking over Baltoro Glacier back to K2, I heard the sound of drums as I approached a large group of Sher's tribesmen. They started singing and I was told in broken English that it was in my honor for saving their brother. They gave me food and water, asked me what Scotland was like and told me I was one of them. I tried to smile but collapsed instead.

WEEK SEVEN

Received an e-mail weather report. Storms coming. I'll die if I go any higher. I haven't slept for days but I don't feel tired. I can't stop, just want to get home. . . . As I walk through the villages wee children put out their little hands and say, "Medicine, medicine," but I have nothing left to give. I am just a dead man walking. I don't know who I am any more. . . .

Why? Why did I go? I did not go to risk my life. I went to find it! A life that is averse to risk is a dangerous illusion. Those who seek to avoid it condemn themselves to dying a million minute deaths every day. Unsure of themselves, they fear the future, are beset by countless, gnawing anxieties that always begin "what if?"

We are the masterpieces of creation, the pinnacle of evolution. It is a crime to squander it, slouched in front of the idiot box night after night, dreaming of a better life yet never possessing the urgency to pursue it. No! I reject that life. I reject complacency and the path of least resistance that leads to a life of rationalized mediocrity. Rather, I pursue what is real, timeless. I lust for experience and vitality, lest my blood dry in my veins. I refuse to die never knowing who I truly was, going to my grave with my music still in me, never discovered, never expressed, with my epitaph being "He Commuted."

We live in an age of unprecedented wealth and abundance, yet we have never been as unhappy. Anti-depressants are amongst the most prescribed drugs, uncontrolled debt spirals as we attempt to buy "meaning." But we were not designed to rest on the laurels earned by our forefathers. We have inherited a paradise and now are bored, spoiled and bloated. We are drowning in plenty, neutered by our cosy existence.

I believe it is our responsibility to do the best we can, to challenge ourselves not only for our own self-respect, but more importantly so that we have the emotional strength to carry someone else if they fall. All we have is each other. Strong communities are made up of strong individuals.

And so I urge you to test yourself and push beyond the

straitjacket of your fears. You will discover riches within yourself that you cannot conceive of, acts of heroism that will take your breath away. You will earn the greatest gift you could ever bestow upon yourself, a deep, enduring self-respect and unassailable self-confidence. Your current stresses will become laughable, the achievement of your heart's desire commonplace, and the person you were put on this earth to be will emerge. You will rediscover the wonders that make us human and be able to look the future in the eye and say, "Do your worst!"

Do it. Pursue life and then you will not have to ask me "Why?" Because by the time you have read this book, you will know.

1

Alexander the Great

Child of the Gods

Alexander the Great stands like a colossus in history, the last great Greek "hero" in antiquity. The undefeatable golden boy who conquered most of the known world in his twenties, died at thirty-two and inspired a legend that would last for ever. He is said to be the greatest secular figure in history, whose influence structured the chain of events that formed the world as we know it, from the cultural foundations of the West to the spread of Christianity and later Islam. He created the world's first single-currency trading empire, founded over seventy cities and was the first leader ever to have a concept of "one world." There are so many lessons that we can learn from his brief and heroic life, and his legend is as compelling for us today as it was for the historical giants such as Napoleon and Julius Caesar who cited him as a major inspiration and tried throughout their great lives to emulate him.

Little Dreamer

Alexander III of Macedon was born in 356 B.C. in Macedonia (present-day Thesalonika in northern Greece), the child of King Philip II and his wife, Queen Olympias. The belief in gods as real entities was a part of everyday reality in the ancient world and Alexander was taught that he was descended through his father from the Greek hero Heracles (Hercules) and through his mother from Achilles, the mythical champion of the Trojan War. In secret his deeply religious mother would tell the young Alexander that his real father was in fact Zeus, the father of the gods. This childhood belief, coupled with the validation that he received later in his life, took on such a profound significance within him that as an adult he even began to refer to King Philip as "my so-called father."

As well as his powerful self-image, Alexander was to be given more than just a vague belief that he was special and destined for greatness, he would receive the inspiration and education that would actually help him to achieve it. It was this unique education that was to give direction to his desires and inspire within him the heroism and superhuman deeds that were to make his name legendary.

At School with Aristotle

The fact that Aristotle was Alexander's boyhood teacher only heightens our impression that he was someone divinely ordained for greatness. It is incredible for us to think that these two men, who would have such a colossal impact on the world, were actually teacher and pupil. Aristotle was without doubt the single greatest influence in Alexander's life. They became very close, so much so that Alexander said that Aristotle was like a father to him. He also said that although his natural father King Philip had given him life, Aristotle had taught him how to use it. Alexander would reward his tutor in a way that neither of them could have imagined: the education that Alexander received helped him to found a Greek empire that enlightened the ancient world and so allowed the ideas of Aristotle to become widespread, gain prominence and change the world, influencing thought to the present day.

Of all the knowledge that Alexander received from Aristotle, there was one gift that he gave him that would have a greater impact on him than anything else and would be largely responsible for his greatest acts of daring and heroism, a simple annotated copy of Homer's *Iliad*, the story of Achilles and the Trojan War. So enthralled was the young Alexander with the exploits of Achilles that he carried the book with him all the way across Asia and even slept with it under his pillow every night.

It seems that as Alexander read the pages of the *Iliad* as a child, he made a pact with the gods that he, like his hero Achilles, would rather trade a long and comfortable life without glory for a short and arduous one that would secure his place in the pantheon of the gods.

In 337 B.C., Alexander's father, King Philip, was brutally assassinated, making Alexander aged only twenty-one, the unopposed ruler of Greece. That is where the story could have ended. But Alexander yearned for an arena worthy of him within which he could prove himself and in 337 B.C. challenges did not come any bigger or harder than that of the

Persian Empire. So, soon after he assumed the throne, Alexander announced a plan that was greeted with both laughter and amazement in all the city states. He was going to fulfill the long-held dream of his father and invade and conquer the Persian Empire of the Great King Darius II, the greatest land empire the world had ever seen. Persia, the superpower of the ancient world, whose lands stretched from Turkey to Afghanistan and upon which "the sun never set." An empire that had literally millions of soldiers at its disposal and enough gold to hire elite Greek mercenaries in their tens of thousands to crush anyone who dared oppose them. The plan was insane, but Alexander was convinced he could do it. In 334 B.C., with an army of only 44,000 men, he set off to embrace his destiny and change history.

The Battle of the Granicus—334 B.C.

At first nobody in Greece or Persia took the threat seriously. Darius had a large army stationed close to where Alexander landed and could have been waiting for him, but instead he allowed the Greeks to land. He then assembled a force of about 40,000 men and positioned them along the banks of the River Granicus. Their plan was simply to stop Alexander from crossing, give him a bloody nose and send him back to Macedonia with his tail between his legs. They were in for a surprise. The Macedonians arrived at dusk. Parmenio, a highly experienced general, who had been one of Alexander's father's right-hand men, advised Alexander to attack in the morning. He urged caution as the river was wide and the muddy banks upon which the Persians were lined very steep, but Alexander, replied that he would be ashamed of himself "if a little trickle of water like this were too much" and decided to seize the initiative and attack immediately.

Alexander, wearing a distinctive double white-plumed helmet, white cloak and shield, led the cavalry attack himself and by sheer force of will, under a shower of arrows and javelins, managed to cut his way up the steep muddy banks of the opposite side of the river. The Persians broke before them and the highly professional Greek troops won the battle almost as soon as it had started. Alexander's excellent generalship combined with his audacious daring had won the first battle for Asia, but his courage nearly brought the campaign to an abrupt end when, in the thick of the fighting, Persian nobles converged on his distinctive figure and very nearly killed him. His advisers begged him to be more cautious but he could not resist leading from the front despite the dangers, or possibly even because of them.

Morale was high after the battle and the army traveled down the coast, occupying the Greek-speaking towns there. Most of them threw their gates open to the invaders, only too happy to be free from Persian rule. Then, when Alexander reached the city of Gordion, an incident occurred so memorable that its name has entered the English language.

The Gordian Knot

Earlier in his career, Alexander had been keen to court the favor of the gods and receive validation of the possibility of the success of his campaign. Before he left for Asia he had consulted the famous Oracle at Delphi. However, on the day he arrived in Delphi the prophetess was not seeing pilgrims.

He sent a message asking if she would make an exception for him but she adamantly refused. Unperturbed, Alexander found her and attempted to drag her to the shrine. Impressed by the passionate young man in front of her, she exclaimed, "You are invincible, my son." Little did she realize the vast consequences her encouragement would have.

And it was to uncover the will of the gods again that Alexander made his way to the ancient city of Gordion. This city had a strange legend attached to it that had its origins in the story of a man called Gordius who emigrated there from Macedonia centuries before. Apparently Zeus declared that whoever drove their cart up to the temple would be declared king. (Bizarre but true.) Gordius inadvertently did this, was crowned, and as a result the town was named Gordion after him. In gratitude to the gods, he left his cart in the temple of Zeus and declared that whoever could untie the incredibly complex knot that attached it would rule all of Asia. Alexander could not resist this challenge, but apparently his closest companions were uneasy. With the whole army waiting expectantly outside, what if he failed? Campaigns could founder on the superstitious fears of soldiers.

The ancient records document the tense atmosphere as Alexander studied the knot. "He stood silent in thought for a while but he couldn't work out how to undo it." Suddenly he stood back, unsheathed his sword and sliced the knot in half. The news was spread that Alexander had fulfilled the prophecy, the soldiers were jubilant and his companions breathed a sigh of relief. To this day, when somebody solves a particularly difficult problem with direct action we say they have "cut the Gordian knot." It was armed with this fresh prophecy that Alexander went to fight.

The Battle of the Issus—333 B.C.

Unlike the battle of the Granicus, at Issus Alexander faced a huge army that was commanded by King Darius himself. Darius's main army outnumbered the Macedonians by more than twenty to one. As usual Alexander led the cavalry charge, launching himself into the thick of the action. This was in direct contrast to Darius, who stood in his chariot behind the front lines, surrounded by hundreds of bodyguards. The most memorable scene recorded from this battle was when Alexander came face to face with Darius, after smashing his way through the Persian lines. The scene was one of total chaos as Alexander and his companions struggled to reach Darius. Many members of the Persian royalty fell trying to defend him before it all got too much for him. He leapt on a fresh horse and fled, leaving not only thousands of soldiers to fight for themselves, but also his wife and family. Persian losses were estimated to be 100,000, the Macedonians, however, lost only a few hundred.

Alexander personally chased the fleeing Darius deep into the night but could not catch him. He returned at midnight sweating, bloody, and bitterly disappointed. His thigh ached from a dagger wound and he decided to have a bath to try and ease his battered body. As he limped into Darius's royal tent, the site that greeted him took his breath away: the room glittered with gold, ornate statues and exquisite fabrics. Even when going to war, Darius surrounded himself with gaudy clutter. As Alexander looked around at the ostentatious wealth surrounding him, he uttered ironically "So this is what it is like to be a king." His words were interrupted by the sounds of hysterical crying and wailing. In the next tent were Darius's mother, wife, and daughters. They were understandably distraught as they awaited their fate but were amazed when Alexander informed them that his war was with Darius not his family. They would be treated like royalty and none of them would be harmed in any way. Alexander never used Darius's family for any political gain, and so chivalrous was his treatment of them that he and Darius's mother, Sisygambis, became very close. So close in fact that, incredibly, she committed suicide years later on hearing of Alexander's death.

Deserts and Divinity

From here, in 332 B.C., Alexander and his army marched down into Egypt, the most powerful kingdom in Darius's empire, where he was crowned pharaoh in Memphis without having to fight a single battle. His time there was marked by two immensely important events: the first would change his life, the second would live on long after his death.

QUEST FOR ETERNITY—THE JOURNEY TO THE ORACLE AT SIWA

In the middle of the western desert was the ancient Oracle of Zeus-Ammon. It was on a par with the Oracle at Delphi in the ancient world and was one of the places where the ancients believed they could ask for the advice of the gods. Even though his campaign was far from over and Darius was still free and raising another army to fight him, Alexander took a whole month off to make a 680 mile detour into the desert to consult the will of the gods. Ancient accounts stress that he was driven there by a strong inner compulsion and a passionate need to have his question answered. But what did he ask and why was it so important to him?

Alexander was the first pharaoh to make the dangerous trek to Siwa. It has been described as a journey into the supernatural. During the two-week expedition across the burning desert to reach the Oracle, his small party ran out of water, and were only saved by a freak storm. They desperately gathered the rain in their helmets and gulped from puddles. Then a vicious sandstorm arose that obliterated the path, and soon even the guides were totally lost. Finally they reached the oasis where the Oracle was located. It was here, in this Garden of Eden in the middle of a desolate wasteland, that Alexander got to ask the two questions that he had carried with him since he was a boy, across the battlefields of Asia and the burning deserts of Egypt. As he stood totally alone in the darkened room of the temple, hundreds of miles from his army, he asked two questions: "Am I a god?" and "Will it be given to me to rule the whole world?" The answer came back out of the darkness: "Yes!" As he stood, his skin parched from the sun, his armor covered in dust, young Alexander of Macedon, the boy-king who had dared to invade the greatest empire the world had ever known, was proclaimed the son of Zeus-Ammon. Achilles had been bettered.

It was a different Alexander who left the temple at Siwa and headed back across the desert. Already the troops who had accompanied him knew that their leader was the son of Zeus. Upon arriving back the news would race through the rest of the army with the energy of a prophecy. The army of Macedon had just become invincible.

But it was the second major action that Alexander took

in Egypt that showed his desire to create a better world. Of all his achievements, it would be the greatest gift he would leave behind after his short life was over.

THE FOUNDING OF ALEXANDRIA—JANUARY 20, 331 B.C.

Alexander was not simply a marauding conqueror. He was an empire-builder, and there is no greater symbol of this than his founding of the city of Alexandria on the Mediterranean coast of Egypt. Geographically and strategically, the location was perfect for the founding of a city. History tells us that Alexander took an active part in the planning of the project and even mapped out the boundaries of the city himself with a trail of barley. Alexandria would grow to have one million inhabitants and become the crossroads of the ancient world, a cosmopolitan center that drew intellectuals, artists, and traders from all over the known world. The Pharos (lighthouse) of Alexandria, one of the Seven Wonders of the ancient world, would be built there, and the city's library would become the largest in antiquity, with over 70,000 books and half a million scrolls.

Alexandria was the first and greatest of over seventy cities that Alexander founded during his campaign, and it became the nucleus of an eruption of ideas and creativity that would change life in Egypt and the ancient world forever. Alexandria and what it stood for, was an integral part of Alexander's vision. It is fitting then that it would become his last resting place.

Back to Business

While Alexander had been founding cities, becoming a god,

and generally achieving his dreams, Darius had been busy raising another army to try and crush them. But deep down he knew that he could not beat the Macedonian and so he tried to negotiate with him instead in the hope that he could buy him off. Unfortunately he did not appreciate the sheer force, size, and momentum of Alexander's vision. Despite the fact that he offered Alexander half of his empire, a huge ransom, and the hand of one of his daughters in marriage, his attempts at bribery were all rejected. At this point Darius must have realized that he had only one option left, the ultimate negotiating gambit, the one that he had been dreading.

The Battle of Arbela—October 1, 331 B.C.

Darius knew that this was his last chance, and he had recruited an army from every corner of his empire. With cavalry that outnumbered Alexander's by more than five to one, and an infantry of 200,000 men to crush Alexander's 40,000, he set out to destroy the Greek invaders and put their young king with his delusions of divinity in his place. Ancient writers recorded the psychological impact that his army had on the Macedonians. "The noise and camp-fires of the Persian camp were so frightening that some of Alexander's generals advised a night attack but Alexander replied bluntly: 'I will not steal victory.'" He would not cheat his destiny.

Darius's cousin Bessus opened up the battle with a charge with his elite cavalry units from north Afghanistan and managed to break through the Macedonian lines. At this point the Persians had a very good chance of winning, but lacking

discipline they continued to ride on to attack the Greek
baggage trains. Parmenio, always the voice of caution, sent an
urgent message to Alexander saying that if reinforcements
were not sent from the front to the rear, their camp and all of
the baggage would be lost to the Persians. Alexander replied
that Parmenio should remember that if they won, they would
not only recover their own baggage but also take the enemy's
and if they lost, then they would not have to worry about
possessions because their "only business would be to die like
brave men." The battle raged on but deteriorated into a
swirling dust bowl as the sand of the Arbela plain was stirred
up by the fury of the combatants. Neither king could see his
commanders to get a clear picture of what was happening. At
this point Alexander decided to use the tactic that had secured
his victory at the battle of the Issus. He would go straight for
the weakest part of his enemy, the heart of the Persian king.

Darius turned to see the Macedonian demon erupt into
view through the dust. Again Alexander and Darius had
come face to face. Alexander threw his spear but just missed
Darius and killed his charioteer instead. As the dying man's
blood covered him, Darius must have felt as if he was living
in a recurring nightmare. He must have known that
Alexander would never stop pursuing him, but rather than
facing his relentless foe, and rallying his men, he decided to
abandon them and run. Despite the fact that the battle could
still have been won, he left his army to die, racing from the
battlefield on his golden chariot, trailing the tattered remains
of the Persian Empire in his wake, with the new, blood-
splattered Lord of Asia in hot pursuit.

The Riches of Persia

On January 30, 330 B.C., after some bitter fighting against the remnants of Darius's forces that they encountered in the mountains outside Susa, the Macedonians reached Persepolis—the capital of the Persians and seat of King Darius's power. Upon entering the magnificent palace, Alexander was overawed by its splendor. He was even more surprised to find the treasure of the Persian kings still intact. In total it came to $80 million (1913 gold values), and it took 700 pack animals to carry it away. Alexander would soon melt the gold down into his own coins, and rather than hoarding it in a vault would use it to fund his campaign and the building of his new empire. He also gave every man in his army the equivalent of a year's pay as reward for their victory at Arbela.

Hunting the King

All of Persia had fallen to Alexander, and its treasures were being minted down into coins for his new empire, but Darius was still free. So after spending the winter in Persepolis, Alexander set off again with a small force determined to capture him. Covering 400 miles in only eleven days, he chased Darius through salt deserts and mountain passes as he fled towards Afghanistan. Alexander's army nearly collapsed with thirst and the heat. Many of his soldiers dropped behind, some exhausted, others as their horses died beneath them, but still the hunt continued, with Alexander, as always, at the front, driving on relentlessly.

The Persian nobility were desperate. They knew that they were hunted men. Darius wanted to continue fighting but the heart and will had left his companions while his soldiers were gradually deserting him. The nobility were paralyzed by what they believed was a plague of bad luck and omens. Driven by their fears, they took Darius prisoner, bound him in golden chains and placed him in the back of a cart in order to conceal their crime from the rest of the army.

By this time Alexander was only a day behind the Persians, and he asked some locals to show him a short cut in order to cut them off. There was one route but it was extremely dangerous, 50 miles with no water, through the desert. Without stopping, Alexander got back on his horse, replaced his weary cavalry with 500 fresh soldiers and raced off into the night. The dash through the desert worked. At first light the Macedonians caught up with the Persian leaders. On seeing them, Bessus tried to force Darius to escape, but honorably he refused to run. The traitors turned on their king and stabbed him with spears, leaving him to die, bound and helpless, in the back of the wagon they had bundled him into. Alexander tore into the camp with only sixty men as the murderers fled into the desert.

The cart carrying Darius's body was found by a Greek soldier at a small spring nearby. He was still alive. The soldier brought him some water in his helmet and comforted him as he died. Greek legend records that with his final words Darius bequeathed his empire to Alexander. As soon as the news reached Alexander that Darius had been found he raced to the scene, but Darius was dead by the time he arrived. His reaction was remarkable. Removing his cloak, Alexander gently wrapped the corpse. Holding the body he sat in silence, stunned at the treachery and tragic death of his adversary, once Lord of Asia. This was not the heroic last confrontation he had dreamed of.

Once Alexander had composed himself he gave orders for the body to be preserved and returned to Persepolis, so that Darius's mother could give her son a royal burial. So compassionate and honorable was Alexander's treatment of Darius's death and his family that within days he had an important new ally enrolled in his elite cavalry division, Darius's brother, Oxathres.

So Persia had fallen, and its "Great King" dead. Alexander had been mocked and laughed at in Greece as a fool and now he had won, his every dream fulfilled. His Great Expedition that had started only three years before was over . . . or was it?

On to the Ends of the Earth

When the army heard that Darius was dead the troops began to celebrate, believing that they were going home, but Alexander had other plans. He summoned the army and explained to them that they were going to go on to the ends of the earth, and find the "Mythical Ocean" that Aristotle had taught him surrounded the world. The journey involved unimaginable hardships: frostbite and altitude sickness as they crossed the Hindu Kush mountains, relentless battles with ferocious Afghani tribesmen, crossing the River Indus into India, and the epic fourth battle of Alexander's campaign against the formidable armies of King Porus on the banks of the Jhelum River. Alexander was wounded repeatedly and his body was racked with dysentery, but his relentless determination never wavered and always he led from the front. But his men were growing weary. The majority of the rank and file did not really know why they were in India in the first place. They believed that the war had been to defeat the Persians and all they wanted to do was go home. In 326 B.C., they mutinied on the banks of the River Beas in the Punjab.

Alexander made passionate speeches imploring them just to go a little further, he appealed to their honor and their greed, but his men had had enough. Perhaps they already knew that Alexander could never stop, that he could have drunk the whole world yet still have been thirsty. Perhaps they had heard that when Alexander was told of the infinite number of worlds in the universe he had started to cry, saying "There are so many worlds, and I have not yet conquered even one."

For three days Alexander waited in his tent, hoping that they would change their minds, but it was to no avail, and so, broken-hearted, Alexander had no option but to turn back. But he had one condition . . . they would go the hard way. What Alexander would never know was that only 370 miles east, three months' march away, was the Bay of Bengal, in Alexander's mind the eastern waters of the Mythical Ocean. He had been so close.

The Long Road Home

Alexander's return from his epic journey across Asia was full of adventure, but two incidents in particular stand out. The first was a further example of his reckless heroism; the second was the first and last time that Alexander would suffer horrendous defeat.

THE SIEGE OF MULTAN

As the Greeks approached the southern Punjab, the Mallians, the fiercest of all the Indian warrior tribes, retreated and awaited them in their formidable fortress of Multan.

Alexander stood before the fortress supremely confident that, like all the others that had gone before, it was only a matter of time before it fell. But something was different this time. The soldiers were hanging back. They had lost their will to fight. Wanting to get home as quickly as possible, they would gladly have left the city untouched. Alexander as always decided to lead by example. Breaking forward from the ranks, he raced to the city wall and, placing a siege ladder against it, climbed up and started fighting alone. Three of his guards followed, but when the rest of the army surged forward, shamed by the example of their king, the ladder broke and Alexander and his guards were stranded on top of the wall. But rather than trying to escape, Alexander leapt down to fight like a demon until he was shot in the chest with an arrow. One of his bodyguards tried desperately to defend his fallen body, using his shield to fend off the hordes of attackers as the other two men were killed beside him. Eventually the army broke through. Alexander meanwhile was carried back to his tent. The arrow had pierced his lung and he very nearly died. However, a week later he rode through the camp to prove he was not dead. As his men cheered wildly around him, Alexander gritted his teeth to hide his agony. His tactic worked. Seeing that the ferocious general was alive, the Mallians and their allies surrendered immediately.

DEATH IN THE DESERT

Alexander suffered only one major defeat in his whole life, but it was not at the hands of a human army. Rather it was at the hands of Nature. In August 325 B.C., as the army took the long road home, they were confronted by the formidable Makran desert. While crossing the unknown territory, they became lost. Wagons had to be left behind, the army ran out of food, and the men were tortured by burning heat, sunstroke, and thirst. Alexander, still suffering from his unhealed wound received at Multan, shouldered the extra agonies of his men. When the horses died he walked; when there was no food he starved; and when some scouts returned with a helmet full of water that they had managed to find, he poured it out in full view of the army, saying, "There is not enough for everyone, and if I drink, the others will faint." Sixty days after entering the Makran desert, the survivors eventually made it out alive, but they left literally thousands dead behind them.

The Clash and Marriage of Cultures

In February 324 B.C., Alexander stopped in Susa on his way back to Babylon. Here unrest amongst his officers and army increased due to the fact that he had adopted Persian dress and was showing favor to the new Persian brigades in the army. Furthermore, he had decided that Babylon would be the capital of his empire. They had thought that their expedition had been to punish and conquer the Persian Empire for their past invasions of Greece, not for Alexander to become its new king and announce that the center of his world would be in Babylonia, not Macedonia. In an attempt to bring the two cultures together, Alexander "ordered" one hundred Macedonian officers to take Persian brides. He and his best friend Hephastion also married the daughters of Darius, whom they had first met as terrified teenagers in the royal tent after the battle of the Issus. Ten thousand Persian women had accompanied the Greek soldiers throughout the campaign, and Alexander ordered his soldiers to marry their companions from this number so as to legitimize their children. He then elevated the women and children to the status of citizens, something the Greeks had never done before. All these actions were intended to bring the two cultures closer together, as, he said, "only in that way could shame be taken from the conquered and haughtiness from the victors." He further astounded everyone when he announced that he would pay off all of his men's debts. The amount was the equivalent of two thirds of the Persian Empire's annual income.

Last Days

Back in Babylon, Alexander began to talk of new expeditions to Carthage, Rome, Arabia and the western Mediterranean. In the midst of all these plans he held a banquet for one of his generals. After it he fell ill with a fever. It persisted, and despite the best efforts of his doctors his condition worsened. A rumor started amongst the soldiers that he was dead, and they besieged the palace, banging on the doors, demanding to see him. His officers tried to stop them but they would not leave. Finally they managed to break down the doors and charged shouting into the room. They were struck silent by the sight that awaited them. Alexander, their invincible king, lay dying on his bed. Ancient chroniclers paint a poignant image of the scene, "They all slowly filed past his bedside one by one, wearing neither cloak nor armor," says Plutarch. Arrian continues: "Nothing could keep them from seeing him a last time and the motive in almost every heart was grief and a sort of helpless bewilderment at the thought of losing their king." The closing line gives us a touching insight into why his men, the common soldiers, were so loyal to him. "Lying speechless as the men filed by, he yet struggled to raise his head, and in his eyes there was a look of recognition for each individual as he passed."

Into the Arms of the Gods

Alexander drifted in and out of consciousness as the fever consumed him, his mind drifting back over the last ten years, so many miles, so many victories, so many challenges overcome. With his dying breaths he made two requests that were close to his heart, that would define who he was. The first was that he be buried with his father: not in Macedonia beside King Philip, but in the desert at Siwa with his true father, Zeus-Ammon. The second was made as he woke surrounded by his generals, a sea of faces, strong and fearless yet marred with tears, asking, "To whom shall you leave your empire?"

Alexander could hardly speak. He thought of Achilles and everything his hero had inspired in him, of the values he had stood for. So when his generals asked again, more urgently, "Sire, to whom will your empire go?" Dying, he whispered the only answer he possibly could: "To the strongest."

His Legacy

Alexander the Great was only thirty-two years old when he died on June 10, 323 B.C. During his short life he changed the course of history. His passionate pursuit of his personal destiny changed the destiny of the whole world and set in motion a chain of events that have formed the world we live in today. The upheaval caused by his epic journey across Asia unleashed vast creative energies and allowed the interaction of peoples and cultures that had previously been impossible. The cities that he and his successors founded, such as Alexandria in Egypt and Antioch in Syria, became the cultural and commercial centers of their day. He awakened the latent masses of the Asian east, and the interplay of commerce and ideas that flowed from there to the West and back again caused nothing short of an economic and cultural explosion. In fact, it can be said that by minting the gold of the Persian kings and putting it into circulation, Alexander single-handedly created the world's first economic boom.

Before Alexander, world civilization had been dominated by Eastern cultures. After him it would shift to the West. Greek became the common language of commerce, trade, diplomacy, and literature, and the economic system that developed after Alexander's death endured until the Industrial Revolution, over two thousand years later. Not only that—he also expanded the concept of what was considered the ends of the earth. Not until the voyages of the Portuguese and Spanish, in the late-fifteenth century, would Europeans believe that they had finally explored further than Alexander had done.

Most importantly, perhaps, was the preservation and

dissemination of Greek ideas from thinkers such as Aristotle and Socrates. Concepts such as democracy and individual freedom would be preserved by scholars in the libraries he built (such as Alexandria) and spread throughout the ancient world.

It was this Hellenistic culture that gave a radical young preacher, Jesus of Nazareth, such a vast audience and the cultural and communications network for it to spread throughout the world. Without it, Jesus's new message would very probably have remained a local Judean phenomenon. Alexander's legacy would have the same effect years later when the Prophet Muhammad began his teachings.

It was this vibrant Hellenistic culture that the Romans inherited when they began to expand their empire around 200 B.C. Through them it spread to Western Europe to be preserved and then rediscovered during the Renaissance and the Enlightenment, and so passed down to us today.

And so in this way, Alexander of Macedon, the boy king who would be a god, became the founder of the West. Little did he know as he charged into battle in his quest for glory that his influence would last for many millennia, and that through that he would achieve his precious immortality.

SECTION TWO: LESSONS
DRIVEN BY DESTINY — WHAT CAN WE LEARN FROM
ALEXANDER THE GREAT

Destiny is not a matter of chance, it is a matter of choice; it is not a thing to be waited for, it is a thing to be achieved.

William Jennings Bryan

Become Consumed By a Dream

Dreams are wonderful things. Dreams inform us as to who we truly are. They seem to come from an eternal, constant part of us that is removed from our daily lives. Dreams are not practical, dreams are not logical and dreams formed the human world that we live in. Every monument, symphony, and great work of art, everything that has been created by human hands first started as a dream. The lives of great people are the products of great dreams. Show me a jaded, bitter person and I will show you someone who has had the dreams kicked out of them. A once great culture in decline is a culture and civilization that has lost the initial dream that made it great and has failed to replace it with one it can believe in. Dreams are like oxygen: we need them to truly live.

If I wanted to see the depths of your soul I would not ask what your name was or where you were from. No, I would ask you what your dreams are, as they would tell me who you really are and where you want to go. The accountant who wishes he was an actor, the marketing director who wishes she could work with orphans and then trek round the world.

But the reason we rarely ask each other what our dreams are is because they are so deeply personal, so revealing; perhaps they are the ultimate intimacy. And the reason we so often avoid asking *ourselves* what our dreams are is because it can be so painful, filling us with a feeling of hopeless yearning or bitter failure.

So let me ask you right now, and don't avoid the question: What are your dreams? Don't judge them, discount them, or over-analyze them; just have fun and let your mind wander. Dreaming should be fun.

OK, here is the next interesting bit. Dreams are incredibly personal. For example, I can confidently say that I have never wanted to be an astronaut, a baseball player, or a doctor. As a result I have absolutely zero motivation to achieve these goals. Our dreams are as different as our talents, and each dream is inspired by our ability to achieve it. The dream that really excites you was not put there by accident or chance. It is an intrinsic part of you, and to deny it is to deny a precious and essential part of who you are. So as you daydream, listen to your feelings and wait for the image that makes your heart race. The dream that sets you on fire. The one that makes you feel as if you are in love. Some people are lucky enough to know exactly what they want to do and have a burning desire to achieve it. The desire is so strong that they cannot conceive of living without it. But for most of us this is not the case and we need a little help to believe we can achieve our heart's desire.

Once you find that image, refine it, let it grow, and bring it to life. Reflect upon it, protect and nurture it, become consumed with it and build your desire to achieve it. In the initial stages dreams can be very fragile things, so it is often best to keep it to yourself until you strengthen your belief, especially if you think that your peers will mock you. If you are like me and you think about something you want to do long enough and fondly enough, then magical things will start happening. You will find yourself being introduced to or sitting beside people who can help you or lead you where you need to go. I bought my dream house, founded my first business, published this book, and achieved countless other cherished dreams all through seemingly chance and random encounters with people who could help me.

This may all seem very simplistic, but the enduring vision of your heart's desire is more important than most people can conceive of. In terms of achievement, all the knowledge in the world is useless unless you have a burning reason to apply it. The man who knows how to do something will always work for the man who knows why. Alexander's invasion of Asia started as he dreamt of being a hero while studying with Aristotle. Dreaming is a serious business. It can change the world. It is both the foundation and the fuel of motivation, and every highly successful person I know has it. So trust me, just for the moment . . . start dreaming.

So if dreaming is so powerful, why does it get such a bad press? In our culture, when somebody says "He is just a dreamer," they are implying that the person will never achieve or do anything. The reason is simple. Dreams are achieved by action, but the vast majority of people give up on them exactly at the moment when they are called to act upon them. Why is this? Why is there such a gulf between desire and action? Why do we let ourselves down and give up on our heart's desire the moment we are called upon to actually do something to achieve it?

The simple answer has to do with belief and desire. If we only dream, but do not actually believe we can achieve, then we will do nothing about it. Secondly, and very importantly, if the obstacles to our goal appear greater than our desire to achieve, we will become disheartened and give up. Some people say that the trick is to make our desire so great that we literally cannot give up and through sheer persistence will eventually make it, but I have always found this answer to be overly simplistic and not very helpful. How many times have you persistently tried your best to achieve something, but no matter how hard you tried, it seemed as if you were banging your head against a brick wall? It would have been a lot easier if somebody had just shown you where the door was. Unfortunately that is the point where so many of us give up. It is here where the second lesson from Alexander's life can help us, a lesson that has been invaluable to me.

Alexander the Great's Motivational Strategy

I believe that Alexander's incredible internal motivation was created by the influence of a trinity of very powerful figures in his life: his father, King Philip; his teacher, Aristotle; and the fictional hero Achilles. Each one of them had a uniquely powerful and positive force in his life. Once we realize what each of them represented to him we can tap into that power and apply it to our own lives. That is when it gets really exciting.

The three principles can work independently of one another and are interchangeable. So, for the sake of illustration, let's look at them one at a time.

FIND A MENTOR

Once we begin to nurture a dream or vision of our future, the inevitable question that arises is "How am I going to achieve this?" How do you become a film director? How do you become a millionaire? How do you become a wonderful parent? All the desire in the world can simply lead to frustration if we do not even know how to get started. It is at this stage that the most powerful thing you can do is to find yourself a trusted mentor. Our ancestors knew all about this. Anxious fathers would take their young sons to the workplace of the local master craftsman and beg him to take their boy on as an apprentice. They knew that studying with a master carpenter or stonemason would be the only way that their child would learn. The greater the master, the greater the heights their child would reach. Unfortunately that system is no longer practiced, and one of the most necessary components in achieving excellence in a given arena is left to chance or accident.

One of the most powerful lessons I learned in business was when I finally found a mentor who I could learn from. For as long as I could remember I had wanted to be a self-made millionaire. I knew why I wanted to and I was willing to work to achieve it. The only problem was that I did not have the first clue how to do it. Sure, I had studied at one of the best business schools, but none of my lecturers were financially independent. They all worked for a living and had never achieved what I wanted to do. They could not teach me to do what they had never done. It was not until I got a chance to work with a couple of guys who had just made their first couple of millions that my eyes were opened.

Getting a chance to work with them on a daily basis, ask them questions about how they got started and how they had felt, see how they reacted to the various challenges they were presented with, took the mystery out of achieving my goal. I saw the people behind the achievements and I began to conceive of exactly how it was done on a day-to-day basis. More importantly, I saw that millionaires were not necessarily superhuman or super-talented, and realized that if they could do it then so could I. Two years later I was well on my way to achieving my dream, and a lot more besides, and my vision had expanded through the wonderful lessons I had learned on my journey. If you are serious about achieving the dreams I asked you to think about previously, then I urge you to seek out the people who have already done what you want to do and learn from them. It worked for me, and I promise it will work for you.

Quality mentors are invaluable. Aristotle taught Alexander the components of greatness, and by giving him his annotated copy of the *Iliad* introduced him to the next essential facet in achieving his dream. He taught him to be inspired by a role model.

BECOME INSPIRED BY A ROLE MODEL

I cannot stress enough that this book is about real concepts and actions that I have learned and applied repeatedly in my own life, from building businesses to climbing mountains. I have no time for motivational pep talks that fall flat on their face the minute they hit the harsh face of reality. As a result I accept totally that the chances of finding a mentor who you can trust and learn from is something that will not necessarily happen overnight. That is why this next lesson from

Alexander is so exciting. This concept was arguably the most powerful motivator in his life and it is something that you have complete and total control over right now. It is the role of Alexander's personal model of excellence, the character he strove to be like all his life, the Greek hero Achilles. Why is this so important? Quite simply because Alexander never met Achilles. He was a character out of a book. And although I would never have said it to Alexander's face, Achilles was a fictional character. He didn't exist, yet as we saw again and again what Achilles represented to him drove Alexander to constantly strive to outdo himself. Alexander made the fiction reality.

Do you see how important this is for you? In every library and bookshop in the country there are literally thousands of books about the lives of the greats. On your way home from work after a bad day, rather than bitching about your boss or succumbing to despair, you could spend the evening in the company of some of the greatest heroes that ever lived and take heart and courage from the challenges they had to overcome. I have read so many books about the lives of characters from history that my mind is literally saturated with countless examples of people overcoming horrendous obstacles and outwitting larger competitors. As a result it has become increasingly harder for me to become despondent or afraid when I suffer setbacks in my life. I have just read too many examples of people who have been through worse and still got there.

Role models embody values, they bring emotional concepts to life and show them in action. One of the most encouraging discoveries we can make is when we read that one of the people that we admire most had to go through exactly the same kind of challenges that we do. The second invaluable quality of role models from history is that they demonstrate that great things are achieved by real people with faults and failings. I know this may sound strange, but I derive a great deal of motivation from reading about my heroes' bad points. Let me explain. I had a good friend who read one of the classic positive-mental-attitude books from America, but amazingly she only read half of it as she said that it depressed her. By reading about how she had to be positive and how she could achieve anything, she simply felt overwhelmed by her own perceived inadequacies and failings. But when we read that someone whose achievements we really admire struggled with a drink problem, had their heart broken or suffered from depression, we realize that we can succeed despite our failings and setbacks. It teaches us compassion and helps us to forgive ourselves, to be philosophical and not take it personally when life kicks us in the teeth. Anyone can be confident and serene when things are going well; greatness and heroism are displayed in adversity. So next time everything goes wrong, rather than panic, smile and think, "How I overcome this is going to make a great chapter in my life story."

Alexander wanted to be a hero, so he picked a heroic role model. What do you want to be? Whose life story could inspire you to achieve it? Read the lives of the people who exhibited the qualities that you desire to emulate, and let the wisdom of their collective lives percolate into your soul. This means that right now, no matter what your background is, you have access to the same source of inspiration that drove Alexander the Great. It means that right now you can carry all the real-life inspiration you need around with you in the shape of a paperback, a sort of mentor in your back pocket if you like. I don't care if it's Batman or Beethoven: just find the right one or ones for you and watch your attitude towards what is possible change with every turn of the page.

But it gets better. You see, if you spend time with the greats and read books about their lives, then not only will you begin to take courage from their experiences and emulate their emotional traits, but you will also have discovered the third powerful motivational secret in Alexander's life. Without ever realizing it you will harness the power of positive peer pressure.

HARNESS THE POWER OF POSITIVE PEER PRESSURE

> He who walks with the wise grows wise, but he who
> keeps the company of fools shall suffer harm.
>
> *Proverbs 13:20*

Humans are social animals. We have evolved to function in a group and rely on others to survive. For our distant ancestors, being cast out of the tribe to survive alone meant almost certain death. As a result our instincts formed to compel us to need acceptance from others. Of course the implications of being rejected by our peers are not so life-threatening today, but our basic instincts are the same and the pressure to conform is incredibly powerful. Responsible parents are obsessed with who their children play with. They know the powerful negative influence that children can have on each other, but those same parents often fail to realize the effect that their peers have on them. While they worry if their child is outside throwing stones, they happily keep the company of visionless morons, yet wonder why life is passing them by. Our friends are very often our mirrors. They reflect back to us who we are, as people with similar beliefs and value attract one another. That is why you are judged by the company you keep. Of course, there are people who are very different from their friends, but on some levels have binding similarities. So ask yourself now, what are the values of your group? What are their aspirations? What attributes do they respect and what do they consider successful? Do you like what you see? What does your peer group say about you? You may be shocked to find that you have never even thought of this. Let me show you how dangerous a lack of knowledge of our peers' values can be.

In his autobiography, Jimmy Boyle, one of Glasgow's most notorious and dangerous gangsters, described one of the turning points in his life. One night, as a young teenager, he was challenged to a "play" fight by a much older boy who was a local gang leader. It was meant to be a bit of fun intended to impress some girls, but Jimmy Boyle was so scared of the older boy that in his terror he saw red and attacked him with such ferocity that the older boy had to beg him to stop. Instantly he gained the respect of all the kids in his neighborhood, and as the story spread he was labelled as "crazy," the greatest compliment you could be given in his environment. He began to enjoy the respect of his peers and so tried to live up to his new reputation. As a result he became the leader of the criminal community and was eventually imprisoned for murder.

Jimmy Boyle was highly intelligent, resourceful, and ambitious, all the attributes necessary to lead a happy, productive life, but because he had adopted the values and goals of his peer group he channelled his talents into achieving goals that ultimately destroyed him. However, what happened next in his life is inspiring for all of us. During his sentence for life imprisonment, Boyle was placed in the "special unit" and encouraged to explore his talents and abilities. Surrounded by different role models and peer values, he began to paint and sculpt, and today is a highly accomplished and famous sculptor. He is no longer Jimmy Boyle the gangster, but Jimmy Boyle the sculptor. Same person, different peer group.

This story indicates a very powerful component of peer pressure, that of "labeling." The turning point in Jimmy Boyle's life was when he was labelled and felt compelled to live up to and behave consistently with his label. Once we have been labelled, our peers will exert considerable psychological pressure to make our behavior remain consistent with that label, without even realizing it. That is our identity within the group that they will feel comfortable with. They will begin to expect that behavior from us consistently. That is why the class clown who decides to become serious finds it very hard to be taken seriously. The fascinating thing is that our expectations of ourselves (and what others expect of us) drive our behavior. We will live up or down to the expectations of those whose opinion we value. If we buy into that label, then it begins to determine our behavior and ultimately who we are. Our label becomes our identity.

This is an extreme example, but have you noticed how you begin to pick up the mannerisms of your friends or subconsciously adopt their patterns of speech? Well, you may not have noticed it but you also pick up their values and thought patterns as well. So ask yourself, where are the behaviors that my peer group value leading me, and is that where I want to go? I am not saying that we should cynically judge people as to whether they will help us achieve our goals. Friendship is infinitely deeper than that, but what I am saying is; do not be blind to the positive or negative effect that your peer group will have on you.

Peer pressure is very powerful and we are all products of our environment, but we can turn this to our advantage. Thankfully it can also work positively. Once we understand its dynamics we can harness the power of positive peer pressure and choose the mental environment that supports us. Rather than being helpless victims, we can use these forces to create a motivating positive pressure in our lives.

Here's another example. I have a childhood friend who has a PhD and is a world authority on geology, as well as being an excellent piano player. He has also suffered all his life from a complete lack of motivation. His success, he says, is because at school he fell in with the right crowd. All his friends used to study most nights, so with nothing else to do he studied as well. As for the piano, his circle of friends formed a band, so he learned the piano otherwise he would have had no mates on Friday nights. Before going to talk at international geology conferences he jokes that if his friends had been gangsters he would be in jail. Even if you have no motivation to do anything, the right peer group can see you through. When I grasped the power that role models and peer pressure exerted in terms of human achievement, I suddenly felt a huge sense of responsibility. I realized that whether I liked it or not I was somebody else's peer, someone else's positive or negative role model. What kind of influence was I exerting on those around me? We are all part of the fabric of each other's lives and our beliefs and

demotivating and is one of the main reasons that people give up despite genuinely giving it their best shot. No matter how motivated you are and how hard you try, if you have the wrong map and directions you will never get there; in fact, you will just get lost quicker. Here's a simple example. Imagine your goal was to be financially independent; well, there are some people who, with the best intentions in the world, would advise you to get a good job and work hard. I, on the other hand, would agree that you will have to work hard, but I would *never* advise you to get a job. Some jobs are fantastic, but not as a way to become financially independent. No, if that is your goal, your best shot would be to set up your own business, and to do that I would advise you to mix with other entrepreneurs. However, if you said to me, "I want to work forty hours a week and never have to think about work at night or weekends," then my advice would be, "Get an undemanding job."

Another name then for a cognitive map is experience, either real or imagined. When you are doing something for the first time and are making loads of mistakes, remember that you are plotting your cognitive map and won't make the same mistakes again. However, a further advantage of the power of mentors and role models is that you can plot your map without having to go through the pain. Rather than falling flat on your face, it is better to listen to or read about someone else who did it. That way you know beforehand where the dangers are. It's a lot less painful and expensive, and you get there a great deal quicker.

But even the best map is useless if you are trying to get to ten different destinations at the same time. If you wish to have crystal-clear clarity as to where you want to go and why, you have to remove the anxiety and confusion of trying to do too many things at once. To achieve this you have to simplify your victory criteria.

Simplify Your Victory Criteria

Modern life is a cacophony of stimuli. Advertisers and the mass media seduce us daily with multiple definitions of success and endeavor to entice us into buying or trying the next fad. All this stimuli is nothing more than one big distraction. If we want to be successful in any particular arena then we need to turn down the volume of the external world and listen to the voice of silence that is within us. Only by focusing on the things that are most important to us in the long term and moving towards them consistently and persistently do we have any chance of reaching them. I come across so many people in business who are passionately enthusiastic about a different idea each month, but the minute they suffer a setback or lose interest they go on to the next one and are excited all over again. The path of least resistance never leads to success. Only by sticking to your goal even when you don't feel like it, will you have any chance of success, and the only way of achieving that sense of determination is to pursue a goal that is truly meaningful to you.

The second dangerous side effect of the prevalence of the mass media is that very often we are sold dreams that we don't really want. We think that our goals are our own but in reality we are conforming to what is expected of us. Magazines tell us that we have to be successful in our careers, have perfect relationships, be amazing parents, incredible lovers, and have an athletic physique with less than 10 percent body fat, and on and on. The debilitating feeling arises that no matter how you are doing in one field there will always be another area where you are failing miserably. If you are busy working on one thing there is the nagging doubt that you are missing out on something bigger and better. In the ancient world, life was a lot simpler, with very few distractions. Alexander knew exactly what he wanted and exactly what to do to achieve it. He also knew exactly how to gauge and measure his success. You either won a battle or you lost it. As a result his actions were reinforced by certainty and clarity. If you want to achieve your goals, it is imperative that yours are too.

So stop now and ask yourself, "Of all the things in the world, what is the one achievement that is most important to me?" After that, ask yourself, "What is the second most important thing?" Create a hierarchy of the five most important things that you want to achieve. Sometimes the answers will take you by surprise, but if you do not know your deepest feelings then there is the risk that you will be working towards a goal that deep down you don't really want. It is imperative that your goals are *yours* not society's, your friends' or your parents'. If the goal is not what you truly want then when you achieve it you may end up feeling unfulfilled and empty.

Once you have done this, take the first answer and ask yourself, "When will I know that I have achieved this?" This question helps you to gauge where you are in terms of your goal. So often in my own life I would say, "I want to be successful in business." But I would never clarify what that actually meant to me. As a result I would never give myself the credit despite the fact that I had achieved so many of my initial goals. Without realizing it I was raising the standard every time I got close to it. This can create the feeling that you are constantly struggling and failing when you are actually succeeding. Clarity of purpose and vision removes doubt and makes us immune to the distracting negative influences around us, but it also does more than that. It helps us to discover our deepest motivation. It helps us to discover the gift behind our goal.

Discover the Gift Behind Your Goal

Alexander wanted to conquer all of Asia, but as we saw from his story, that was not his deepest motivation. Deep down he believed that by living a heroic life he could become a god. It was his means to an end. You may not realize it, but it's the same with you. Your goals are only really a means to an end. So right now I am going to show you how to achieve your goal without even leaving your seat.

In the last section I asked you to list your goals in order of what is most important to you. Now let's go a stage further. Take your most treasured goal, and ask yourself, "Why?" You've probably never asked yourself that either have you? The answer is always very revealing. Here are some classic examples. If I achieve my goal, then . . .

- People will respect me.
- Everybody will like me!
- I will feel secure.
- I will feel good about myself.
- God will be pleased with me.
- Nobody will be able to laugh at me.

- My parents will be proud of me.

Sometimes we have to go deeper again and ask, for example, "Why do I need to be successful before people will respect me?" or "Why do I need financial wealth to feel secure?" All sorts of deep feelings can then come out which make us look at ourselves in a different light. Don't you think it's a bit hard on yourself to say, "I won't like myself until I am rich," or "I won't respect myself until I am the managing director?"

These questions are truly revealing and can be uncomfortable, but they remove the dangerous illusions that can be behind the reason why we think we want our particular goals. They illuminate what we really want and can save us from pursuing some irrelevant goal when deep down all we crave is the ability to like ourselves. Here's a personal example. Years ago I wanted a BMW sports car. At the time it was the answer to all of life's problems. Well, I got it, and the next day I was sitting in a traffic jam feeling particularly angry and stressed about something unimportant, and as I looked down, I saw my sad little reflection on the shiny BMW badge on the steering wheel. Once I learned the things we have been discussing I realized deep down all I had really wanted was to feel in control of my own destiny. The car was an empty symbol of that. Now that I have "allowed" myself to feel that way, fancy cars are totally unimportant to me.

The second profound truth that these questions reveal is that in our comfortable society, the drive behind our goals is all emotional needs: self-respect, pride, admiration, security, etc. This realization is liberating and can effect profound change in our lives. It means that we can reward ourselves

with what we really want, the feelings we wish to have . . .
right now. Sitting right where you are, you can create
feelings of self-respect, happiness, confidence, or whatever
emotional state it is you crave. The irony is that once we feel
the emotions that we think our external goals will bestow
upon us, it actually makes the achievement of them so much
easier. That is what I meant when I said I could show you
how to achieve your goal right now. Unfortunately, I know
that this is sometimes easier said than done, and being told
to be confident is actually quite irritating. In order to acquire
these emotional attributes, you will have to practice the
single most important discipline in going from where you are
now to where you want to go. You will have to constantly
work on your self-image.

Work on Your Self-Image . . . Constantly

All appears to change when we change.

Henri Amiel

The universe is change; our life is what our thoughts
make it.

Marcus Aurelius Antonius
(A.D. 121–A.D. 180) *Meditations*

Are you a good dancer? Think about it for a minute.

Now whether the answer was yes or no, what information did you use to determine it? Without you being aware of
it, your mind showed you various images of you gyrating in
the past, and from that information you decided whether or
not, in your opinion, you were a good dancer. Perhaps your
mind processed the reactions and comments of those you

had danced with or compared yourself to others dancing. But I bet you didn't put this book down, get up, and start dancing round the room to help you decide. No, you used the one thing that you always use to determine every aspect of your opinion of yourself . . . your memory.

For most of us, our ability to dance is pretty unimportant. So here's another question: "Are you intelligent?" Now, your mind is racing through memories of being told you were stupid by old schoolteachers. "But wait," you say, "I scored six straight As on my exams. That is not my opinion. That is a fact, proof that I am intelligent."

Really? Maybe that just means that you are good at studying, or that the exams were particularly easy that year. Do good exam results definitely mean you are intelligent?

Here's another example. If you work for a living, imagine changing your current job for one that you are sure you could easily get. How much would you earn? Now multiply it by four. How did you react? Did you say, "I could never earn that?" Now imagine you saw an advertisement for a job that paid half of what you currently earn, would you go for it? Probably not, because even if it could cover your monthly outgoings, it would be "beneath" you. The above examples give you a very accurate insight into your self-image with regard to what you are worth financially.

The point that I am making is that our perception of who we are is purely an opinion, an idea. Our opinions determine our behavior. We then take our actions or the reactions of others to be evidence that we are stupid or unattractive or whatever. The concept or opinion we have of ourselves is the single most important determining factor in how well or badly we do in life, whether we will be happy or miserable.

Our thoughts dictate our experiences and in no area is this more relevant than the pursuit of our goals and dreams.

The fascinating thing about a person's self-image is that most of us don't know we have one and think that our opinion of who we are is reality. No matter how negative or disempowering a person's self-image is, they are actually very attached to it. Try telling somebody who is convinced that they are stupid that they are actually intelligent and they will argue with you that you are wrong. And they will have loads of examples to prove that they are in fact an idiot.

Where did you get your opinion of who you are? It is nothing but a random selection of memories of experiences and comments from other people that you choose to remember from your past. It comes from the influence of your peers, parents, and friends. The most important possession you have came about through chance. Some of our ideas about ourselves are minor—such as whether you like wine or not—but others, such as what you are capable of and what you expect from yourself, literally determine the quality of life you will lead. Everything, from your job, your lover, your expectations of the future, to your dress sense, is determined by your self-image. If you are serious about achieving your goals it is vitally important that you grasp this and commit to taking control of how you perceive yourself.

Unfortunately it is not going to happen overnight. This is not a quick-fix book. Our culture is becoming obsessed with fads: Lose twenty pounds in a week! Develop a winner's attitude in a day! If you are serious about creating a dignified life and achieving your goals you must detach yourself from this fickle nonsense and make a commitment to yourself.

When we begin to examine the thoughts that make up who we are, some of our discoveries can be upsetting. We discover why we could never progress in our career or stand up for ourselves, why our relationships break up. We begin to see that our thoughts create repeated patterns of behavior in our life. We go through the same worn-out pantomime over and over and the sobering realization sets in that we will continue to play that part and go through those same experiences until we change the thoughts that cause it. The reason is simple. A computer can only run the program that is in it. If we have been programmed to be miserable, then being told to cheer up is not only very annoying, but also next to impossible. It's like being told to suddenly speak a foreign language. You simply do not know how to do it, but with time and commitment you can learn.

Repeated behavior can be an excellent indicator of our most dominant beliefs. By examining the same things that happen over and over in our lives we can begin to identify the thoughts that cause us to scream, "Why does that *always* happen to me?" By changing the underlying thoughts that cause the experiences that make us unhappy, we can free ourselves from them, rather than feel angry or depressed every time history seems to mysteriously repeat itself in our life. However, remember that you are a product of your past role models, environment, and of all the negative debris that you have picked up over the years. It took you years to learn and refine who you are, and it will take time for you to identify and throw off some of the opinions about yourself that have been holding you back. So be gentle with yourself. Only by treating yourself with compassion and forgiveness can you gradually escape the thoughts that are binding you.

Make an enduring commitment that you will free yourself from the yoke of the past and that no matter how long it takes, you will never sell yourself down the river because of a poor self-image.

Alexander the Great was fortunate enough to be brought up in an environment that helped him to form a very powerful self-image that supported his ambitions, but even he had to work on his self-image in order to give him the belief and the confidence that he could actually achieve the massive goal he had set himself. Throughout his early years he regularly sought out soothsayers to ask the gods if he would be successful. This need was so great in him that he nearly died crossing the desert to consult the Oracle at Siwa. Only when he finally received that external validation did he actually stop consulting such people. This behavior is mirrored by many successful people who achieve great things. No matter how confident you are, if you set yourself a huge goal you will always be aware of the difference between who you are now and the person you will have to become in order to achieve it. And that is why the need to have a goal that you passionately desire to achieve is so important. You will never go through the pain or effort of changing your self-image unless you have a reason to do so. You will never change your opinion of yourself unless that opinion can no longer provide you with something you deeply desire. If you want to achieve great things, the first step is to begin building a great self-image. For an arduous journey you need a robust vehicle. I cannot stress the importance of this enough. When I am going on an expedition I work on my body. When I am expanding my business I work on my mind.

If you work in a job that you hate with a boss who puts you down and co-workers who make your life a misery, very often it can make you feel trapped. Your evenings are spent worrying about it or trying to forget about it. So often we lack the confidence or the belief that we can get out of the very situation that is causing us so much pain. If this is the case, then start to create mini victories for yourself outside the workplace in areas in which you have control. If you cannot progress at work then commit to building your self-image outside of work. Everything you do in your life affects every other area of it. Tiny victories have a habit of building into big victories. They create exciting momentums that eventually transform your life. Just start where you are and take the next step, no matter how small or humble. Forget about the fact that you don't have the confidence to achieve your bigger dreams; just take the next step. Do whatever interests you outside of work. Set goals at the gym, take some night classes, join a football team, anything you like, but if you keep setting small challenges for yourself and building up your confidence, self-worth, and self-belief, one day you will suddenly see that you have outgrown your current situation and you will just walk out the door and never look back.

I built my businesses and climbed some of the most dangerous mountains in the world in this way . . . one step at a time. It took me years, but when I look back now at jobs I had when I was younger, I either laugh out loud or shudder at the thought of still being stuck there. Despite all the multimillionaires, famous climbers, and musicians that I know, the thing I admire the most is the person with no friends, money, or opportunities who is stuck in a dead-end job but has the courage to do what they fear and take that small step to build a better future for themselves. That is where true heroism is revealed and my heart swells with pride when I see it. When you reach your goal and look back at where you started from, it is that first step that will make you most proud of yourself. And remember, the courage to take that step, then the next and the next, is all you really need. It will take you to the ends of the earth if you want it to.

Construct a Belief in the Inevitability of Your Positive Destiny

When you set out to achieve something of worth it is inevitable that you will suffer setbacks and be knocked off course. When this happens it is essential that we believe that the desired outcome is still possible, that we expect to achieve our goal. The greater the belief in the inevitable achievement of our goal, the less the setbacks will bother us. This certainty also massively reduces stress and takes the worry out of our trials. The interesting thing is that the difference between the person who marches on regardless and the person whose efforts are besieged by doubt is only really a question of belief, and no matter how powerful a belief it is, it is nothing other than a thought, an extension of our self-image. That is why I use the phrase "construct a belief" as it does not necessarily need to be true. The person with unshakable faith does not know that it is true either; they simply believe it to be so. So creating this positive belief is a very useful mental illusion. You may find that statement bizarre, but what many of us do not realize is that most of our beliefs are illusionary, such as "People don't like me," or

"Things never work out for me." Once we understand this, we can construct positive beliefs rather than labouring under negative ones that ultimately are merely opinions we have chosen to cling on to. This certainty gives you the courage and confidence to align your actions with your deepest needs and highest aspirations.

So right now picture the outcome of your goal and take note of how it makes you feel. Visualizing your goal does two things. First, it flushes out your fears. If you find that you can't see it or feel uneasy about it, then the chances are you don't really believe your goal is possible or that you deserve it. Second, if you can't visualize it then do you really know what you want? It is hard to hit a target that you can't see.

Believing in the inevitability of our positive destiny makes us cheery in adversity and helps us to maintain a positive resolve, as we know that no matter what happens we will get there in the end.

Align Your Actions with Your Deepest Needs and Highest Aspirations

In the late nineteenth century a debate raged between two schools of thought in the criminal justice fraternity. One group believed that the role of prisons was to rehabilitate prisoners, whereas the other, more established group believed that the sole purpose of prison was to provide unrelenting punishment for the inmate. Here is one of the more interesting punishments the latter group devised. Attached to the wall in the corner of a prisoner's cell was a circular barrel containing pebbles. A handle protruded from it. When it was turned, the pebbles were scooped up and moved from the top of the barrel to the bottom. Turning the handle served no purpose whatsoever, other than moving the pebbles. Prisoners were ordered to spend the whole day turning the handle without a break. The goal of this work was to completely break the spirit of the inmate. The purposelessness of the whole exercise robbed them of their self-esteem or any feeling that they were achieving or contributing anything. The utter futility of the labor even drove some of them mad.

This feeling of futility and lack of over-riding purpose is what causes many people to feel utterly depressed by the job that they go to day in, day out. As in the above example, the feeling that our labor is contributing nothing not only makes us depressed and drains our energy, it also robs us of any motivation that we can muster. In my own companies I have often been amazed at the fact that some people who, at work, would appear to be unmotivated and even lazy will gladly run their guts out on a soccer field in the freezing rain after work and never expect to be paid for it. The challenge for me is to find a way to connect that person's role in the company with the passion that drives them to give so much of themselves on the sports field. As we discussed earlier, having a dream or goal gives every action that takes us towards it, meaning and purpose. However, when we look deeper into the factors that drove Alexander the Great, we see that it was not simply that he had a goal that drove him but that his goal fulfilled his deepest needs and highest aspirations. The fulfillment of his dream not only fulfilled his financial needs or his career ambitions, but was the fulfillment of his deepest sense of who he was and what he aspired to be. In his religious culture, conquering Asia even fulfilled his deepest spiritual needs and ensured his immortality. How motivated would you be if you believed that achieving your most difficult goal would ensure your spirit's immortality? It changes the perspective, doesn't it? This connection with our goals and our highest values is essential for one simple reason. It gives our life something that many of us are sadly missing in today's society . . . It gives our lives meaning. To pursue our goals heedless of this concept very often leads to a sense of disillusionment once they have been achieved.

I am fortunate to know a lot of people who have achieved huge successes in their lives. Of the business people I know, once the initial elation of success had worn off, a significant number began to say similar things:

- It's not what I thought it would be. I feel empty.
- What has my life been about? What was all that work for?
- I'm bored.

They had achieved financial success on a huge scale but had neglected to align their work to something that they could derive deeper meaning from. I don't think it's necessary for us all to go and work in the Third World in order to find meaning. It's much more practical for most of us to find a way of seeing how what we do on a day-to-day basis contributes to what we value in a deeper sense. Many of us make an invaluable contribution to society but have not made that connection with our seemingly mundane tasks. If you discover that this is impossible in your current position, then this discovery can often give you greater conviction to move.

There are so many factors that influence us today that

sometimes we find ourselves with feelings of conflict and tension within us. Sometimes our current behavior is in conflict with the religious upbringing we had as children or other values we learned from our parents. We may have intellectualized that we no longer hold those values, but a deep part of us still does. As a result we can feel unexplained tensions and conflicts within us. When it comes to achieving our goals, this clash of values makes the achievement of them next to impossible. Here is an example. Imagine your goal was to become financially wealthy and you were shown a guaranteed way of making a fortune in months. All you had to do was kidnap children from the Third World, kill them, and sell their organs. Simple. Would you do it? Of course not. Why? Because you would be going against your values and our culture's most cherished concepts of what is right and wrong. Imagine you did do it and made a fortune, how would you feel about yourself? I call this the Judas complex, where we sacrifice our moral values for external success. It's a sure route to emotional disaster. Here's another example. Imagine you had the same financial goal and you had a chance to discover a cure for all the diseases in the world and an end to world poverty. The only catch was that you personally would not take a penny. Would you do it? I think you would. Personal financial gain could never touch that level of contribution and personal satisfaction.

So this lesson from Alexander calls us to examine our souls further. It asks us to ensure that our goals and actions are aligned with our deepest desires and values in life. By doing so, the achievement of them becomes so much more effortless and graceful.

Alexander showed us the key to a life of fulfillment and

enduring motivation, but he did much more than that, he showed us the secret of how to act as if it were impossible to fail.

Act As If It Were Impossible to Fail

I never used to like this phrase. It always struck me as a motivational cliché and prone to encouraging behavior that was akin to reckless abandonment. I know what the author was getting at, that by acting with complete boldness we would achieve our goals. There is wisdom in this, but I can confidently say that in my past, had I acted as if it were impossible to fail, I would either be bankrupt or frozen to death on a glacier. Success comes from having faith in yourself and what you are doing but by also being acutely aware of the possibility of failure and taking steps to avoid it. However, once I had studied the life of Alexander the Great I was repeatedly struck by how he did seem to act as if it were impossible for him to fail. This psychology fascinated me. Once I looked at his behavior from a motivational psychology point of view I began to discover the inner dynamics that caused this. I began to understand that in Alexander's mind, by acting the way he did, he literally could not fail.

As we know, Alexander's deepest motivation was to be heroic and live a life like his role model Achilles. By proving himself he believed that he would receive his ultimate reward, he would be deified and become immortal. The arena within which he chose to prove himself was the invasion of the Persian Empire.

How then was it impossible in his mind for him to fail?

Through his sheer boldness and often reckless courage Alexander inspired his troops and terrified his enemies. This behavior resulted in victory on the battlefield and took him closer to proving himself as the successor to Achilles. This in Alexander's mind equaled success.

However, the very act of charging headlong into battle and taking incredible risks with his personal safety also proved him to be a hero. If he had been killed in action he would have proven again that he was a worthy successor to Achilles. Again in Alexander's mind this equaled success.

Therefore, whether he won or lost, as long as Alexander continued to act heroically, it was literally impossible for him to fail.

How is this relevant to your life? Its impact is dependent on you understanding your values and highest aspirations, as we examined earlier. If you remain motivated by external symbols such as prestige cars and homes that you believe will make people admire you, you may achieve your goals but your efforts will be dogged by a fear of failure, as success will only be measured in the acquisition of your goal. Furthermore, people who measure success in external symbols often find it hard to enjoy them as they are scared that they will lose them. Also as discussed above, they are often prone to feelings of emptiness and futility once they have achieved their goal.

This revelation changed my life. It freed me from the trap of judging my actions solely on whether they were externally successful or not. I realized that as long as my actions fulfilled my most cherished values, simply taking action in the direction of my goals meant that I was living a successful rich life, rich with meaning. Simply taking action made me, in my mind, successful. This realization gave my actions an energy and focus that made the process of achieving my goals much more enjoyable and the attainment of them much easier.

This realization leads us to a more sophisticated and mature understanding of what motivates us. It helps us transcend the momentary enthusiasms that can consume us as we run around pursuing external material goals like dogs chasing sticks. By devoting ourselves to a philosophical ideal, we can become motivated by a deeper vocation and discover real purpose and meaning in our lives. This insight into Alexander's psychology helps us understand why throughout his life he appeared totally uninterested in material wealth. His behavior reveals the profound truth that true wealth is the pursuit of fulfilling your goals and dreams.

True Wealth Is the Pursuit of a Goal and a Dream Fulfilled

As we develop our self-image and self-esteem, we begin to notice that the things that are important to us start to change. One area where this is particularly pronounced is in the realm of material wealth and money. Once our motivations are animated by our deepest values, we begin to see material wealth in a totally different light. It becomes a by-product of who you are, of your high personal standards, not your reason for living. Of course you can enjoy it, but you certainly do not need it. The idea of needing material wealth and a fancy car becomes laughable, the need to display wealth in an attempt to impress others, grotesque. But more than this, we realize that the addiction to wealth and status is itself a golden cage. It can actually have a restricting effect on our creativity and courage. By making us need status and trinkets, we begin to fear losing them, and this fear can sap the very attributes we need to be truly successful. In the Alexander story, King Darius was infinitely wealthier in material goods than Alexander, but greatness is not measured by the size of your bank balance. He was so addicted to the role of being the cosmic king that it became his undoing. Alexander's wealth was of the spirit; the fact that he became the richest man in the world was coincidental. The trappings of success were a distraction to him. You cannot live with that level of determination and energy and not be successful. Darius had so much to lose that every time he faced Alexander on the battlefield he ran away. The irony is that his fear of losing resulted in him losing everything.

This is as true today as it was then. Here's a modern example. A good friend of mine is a world-famous musician. When he wrote his first album he had nothing and lived in a studio. It was incredibly successful and as a result he acquired a Mercedes, a cool flat, and all the other trinkets that go with monetary success. We met for a drink while he was writing his second album and he confessed to me that he was depressed and was having real difficulty writing. "Every time I try to write I keep thinking that if this album is not successful, I will lose my house and the critics will pan me." Only by reconnecting with what was really important to him and realizing that his true passion was art and not money was he able to rediscover his initial inspiration.

Exactly the same thing happens in business. Large bloated corporations can be eaten alive by younger, hungrier entrepreneurs who have nothing to lose and as a result are not afraid of losing their fancy titles and prestige cars. Once you have satisfied your basic human needs of food and shelter and removed the anxiety of paying your bills, then money really is not the key to happiness. I know a lot of self-made millionaires who after a year of lounging about inevitably start up another business and begin all over again. They realize that it is the pursuit of building and creating something, of contributing and pouring themselves into a challenging project that makes them happy. We are all very aware of the term "poverty trap" but there is also a syndrome that I call the "affluence trap." It can ensnare you once you have a little success and become scared to move in case you lose it. It will sap your courage and your desire to strive, but there is an antidote and that is to learn to thrive on hassle and hardship.

Thrive on Hassle and Hardship

When I was learning to sky-dive in the Australian outback I asked the instructor if there were any books that I could study or information that I could use to prepare for it. He just smiled and said in his laid-back drawl, "Naw, mate, you'll just have to jump." A couple of days later, as I stared down at the desert from 14,500 feet up, the last thing I wanted to do was leap out into the clouds, but there was no turning back, so I jumped. All the reading in the world could never have expressed the sensation of falling at 100 miles per hour through the air. Once I landed, the sensation of achievement was incredible and my fear had evaporated.

Everything that we have talked about so far is designed to lead up to that moment, the time you are called upon to act, to jump. You can have an excellent peer group, mentors, and role models coming out of your ears, but if you still can't bring yourself to act when your chance comes then you will never move forward in your life. You will just stagnate in your knowledge. This is not a bad thing; it just means you have to keep building your self-image, but one of the quickest and surest ways of conquering your fear is to just do the thing that scares you. I know it sounds simple, but it is true.

One of the reasons people procrastinate and delay is because of the fear of the hardship, challenges, and hassles that they imagine might happen once they start. Well, I have a piece of news for you that you may not like: if you decide to go after a big enough goal, the hardships will definitely come. It is totally naïve to hope they won't and pointless to be shocked when they arrive. Trying to achieve something without the will to confront problems is a bit like trying to go for a swim without getting wet. It's part of the deal.

I was at the launch of a new technology company and the director asked me if I had any advice I could give him. With the best intentions I explained, "Your job as the director of a new company is to solve problems. Once you've solved them you will get bigger problems, then even bigger ones. The bigger the problems you can handle, the bigger your company will become." He looked shocked, and said, "Well, thanks a lot," and stormed off. Incidentally, that is exactly what my mentor taught me and he was right. Three months later the new technology company had spent all its money and gone bust. Perhaps he thought running a company was about going to launch parties and being the big man in the office, but he obviously didn't grasp the concept that he was there to solve problems.

Some people when they set out to achieve a goal seem to think that challenges and setbacks are unusual and feel indignant when they occur, but what they fail to realize is that they are an essential part of the process and actually make the journey more interesting. Imagine you were renting a film and the description on the back of the box said "The hero finds a map to a hidden treasure, so he gets in his car, drives there, digs it up and comes home, end of story." Would you rent it? No, you want to hear that he is attacked and kidnapped, then escapes only to find there is a mistake on the map and a beautiful woman has the key, etc. Great stories are all about characters overcoming considerable odds and being transformed in the process. If you avoid problems all your life you will have one hell of a boring life story and you will never move on. Furthermore, people who run from their problems tend to get chased by them. Life becomes a bully and pushes them around.

The amazing thing about hassle and problems is that they never seem as big the second time round. If you successfully deal with them the first time, the second time you won't even notice them. The experience will have formed your cognitive map. By passing the test you graduate to the bigger problems. It's like doing push-ups: one week you struggle to do five, a month later you are pushing fifty. Your emotions and ability to handle stress are exactly the same: push them and they get stronger. That is the wonderful thing about our goals and dreams. We create them but they also create us. The challenges sculpt us into what we need to become to achieve them. That is why it is so important to build your self-image. If you become bigger than your challenges then they are not so daunting and you can move on to bigger and better things. What most people who run from challenges don't understand is that our society rewards those who solve the biggest ones. Huge success is simply the solving of big problems. Anyone can sweep the streets, but what if you developed a cure for cancer? Your name would go down in history. That is why I personally admire Alexander the Great so much. He shunned the easy life and thrived on tests and challenges, and his will to do what his enemies would not, made him hugely successful. He taught me to actually enjoy overcoming hardships rather than feeling resentment and moaning, "Why me?"

So don't fear your hardships and hassles; welcome them as signposts along the way that help you become who you need to be. If you look hard enough you will see that they actually contain the seeds of greatness. One of the key attributes of greatness is to allow the defeated to keep their dignity.

Allow the Defeated to Keep Their Dignity

When you beat somebody, never gloat or go out of your way to mock them. The reason that Alexander managed to build such a large empire so quickly was by turning his enemies into loyal allies once they had been defeated. By aligning the vanquished to his cause he united various diverse cultures rather than forging an empire full of humiliated people seething with resentment. There have been many conquerors in history, but Alexander's treatment of the defeated is one of the main reasons that he is remembered as great. How can we apply this in our lives?

The moment a person has been beaten they are at their most vulnerable. If we treat them with respect and allow them to save face, by being humble in victory, the defeated can often begin to think that they were wrong to have competed with us in the first place. Deep down they will also be very grateful that we have not humiliated them, especially if it is in public. If you need that person to help you in the future you will find the task a lot easier if you have treated them with respect. If you have gloated over your victory, then the chances are you will have created an enemy for life and the first chance they get they will have their revenge.

When I see somebody doing a little victory dance and taking rapturous pleasure in the discomfort of their defeated opponent, my first reaction is always to think that the contest has obviously been very difficult for them and that they lack confidence. Excessive glee is usually an indicator of a low self-image. It also gives the impression that the victory, was obviously a huge deal for them, so it gives us an insight into their capabilities. If they are calm and magnanimous then they give the impression that they had almost infinite reserves to draw on, that the competition was not that stressful. This can put the opponent and observers off ever wanting to compete with them in the future. Of course with all your hard work you deserve to congratulate yourself, but just make sure it is not at the expense of another person. Dignity in victory as well as defeat will give you a reputation of honor among your peers which will be invaluable to you in the future. It also means that they will be a lot gentler on you when it is your turn to be defeated.

Know When to Stop

When we read back over the events of Alexander's short life and grasp the sheer weight of the momentous achievements that he was responsible for, we can see why he has been called "the greatest secular figure in history." This realization makes it all the more inconceivable that Alexander would have considered himself to be a dismal failure. Contemporary historians recorded that he had no idea what to do with the rest of his life when his troops forced him to turn back, and it has even been suggested that his illness was brought on by excessive drinking as he sought to drown his despair. The tragedy of Alexander's life is that the very internal motivation that drove him to achieve on such a colossal scale also made him incapable of stopping. Internal motivation is an intensely personal affair and it is important that we develop the ability to stand outside of ourselves and try to see our achievements from an objective stance. By doing this we can allow ourselves to feel happy in our achievements and prevent ourselves from feeling like failures when all around us are in awe of our successes.

Conclusion

Studying Alexander has taught us the deepest concepts of motivation and given us a clearer insight into how to lead a fulfilled and passionate life, rich in meaning and contribution. However, there is another way to achieve the same motivation levels and produce the same results without having to do any of the above. If you are poor, hungry, and desperate and have to succeed because you will be killed if you don't, if you need to succeed because you literally have no choice and nowhere else to go, then you will know what it was like for our next character—you will have tapped into the dark side of motivation and have the same ferocious drive as Genghis Khan.

2

Genghis Khan

Section One: History

The Horsemen of the Apocalypse

In 1211, as if from nowhere, a lethal force was unleashed upon the earth. To the medieval mind it was as if the Four Horsemen of the Apocalypse were abroad bringing Death, War, Famine, and Pestilence to all they encountered. Detesters of cities and city-dwellers, they swept across the world like an all-engulfing black tide, a swarm of locusts devouring all in their path. Stunned into helplessness by the ferocity and speed of the onslaught, the medieval Europeans believed that the horsemen were demons who had been sent to punish them for their sins. Churchmen spoke of monsters with dogs' faces devouring babies and eating the genitals of their victims, and the churches were crammed as they awaited their doom. The source of the world's terror was the Mongol hordes, and so advanced were they in the art of bringing death that it seemed as if they had come from outer space to destroy humanity.

Never in human history had so much land been conquered so completely, so quickly. In less than fifty years the Mongols had created an empire that stretched from Korea to the River Danube, an empire four times the size of that of Alexander the Great. Almost a third of the Earth's land surface was under their command, and still their empire continued to grow. This is even more incredible once we understand that the emergence of the Mongol nation can be attributed to the iron will of just one man, their founding father and guiding spirit. It was not until his successor commissioned his story to be recorded that the Mongols actually appear in any written record. The *Secret History of the Mongols* tells of the trials of Temuchin, or "Blacksmith," the young man who would use the hardships of his early life to sculpt himself into the formidable Genghis Khan.

"I Was Raised on the Steppes"—The Childhood of Genghis Khan

To say that Temuchin's chances of rising to greatness were slim would be an understatement in the extreme. He was the oldest son of Yosegei, a minor clan chief, and Ho'elun, whom his father had abducted from another clan chief. It was Mongol tradition for a mother to name her child after an event or person whom she felt was significant to the birth. So Temuchin, born in 1167, was named after a Tartar chieftain whom his father had just killed in battle. At the tender age of nine, Temuchin was taken by his father to live with the tribe of his future bride, Borte. On his way home Yosegei met a group of horsemen and stopped to eat and drink with them. Three days later his horse walked back into camp with

Yosegei draped over its back. The horsemen had been Tartars and, recognizing Yosegei as the man who had killed their chief, had laced his drink with poison. He died in agony later that night. No sooner had Temuchin begun to settle in with his new in-laws than he received the news of his father's murder. As if this was not hard enough, his father's clan were unwilling to have a nine-year-old as their leader. Despite his mother's pleas, they abandoned them to join a rival clan, leaving Ho'elun alone with five children and two step-children, all under the age of ten, to fend for themselves. In the harsh terrain of the Mongolian steppes it was effectively a death sentence. Temuchin lived as an exile, surviving kidnap attempts, sub-zero temperatures, and malnutrition until he reemerged into Mongol society at the age of sixteen. Seven years after he had first met her, he rode into the camp of Borte, his betrothed. Temuchin had returned from the dead to claim his bride.

Temuchin's ability to survive had demonstrated that he was a force to be reckoned with, and shortly after his return he set about reclaiming the leadership of the tribe that had been taken from him. His experiences had taught him that if he wanted to achieve this and be less vulnerable to the chaotic allegiances of the steppes, he would need the support of a strong ally. The logical choice was Toghril, the leader of a tribe called the Kereyids, who had been the *anda* of his father. The concept of an *anda* was unique to the Mongols and was an oath of allegiance sworn between two men, like blood brothers. Temuchin himself, at the age of ten, had already become the *anda* of a boy from another tribe called Jamuqa and the two had become inseparable allies. Toghril was delighted to support the son of his former blood brother and agreed to help Temuchin regain his birthright. But just as the preparations were being made and it seemed as if things were at last going Temuchin's way, his camp was raided by marauding horsemen of the Merkid tribe. Temuchin barely managed to escape, along with his mother, brothers and sisters, and in a bitter replay of history fled into the mountains. Once safe, however, he discovered to his horror that Borte had been abducted and that the leader of the raiding party had taken her as his wife. However, unlike the first time when disaster had befallen Temuchin as a child, this time he had some powerful allies. Toghril, his new patron, remained true to his word, and upon hearing of the raid raised an army under the command of Jamuqa.

Temuchin descended upon his wife's abductors like a demon, and the campaign to rescue her was a total success. The Merkids were defeated and Borte was returned unharmed. But one fact overshadowed the newly-weds: Borte returned pregnant. To his credit, Temuchin raised the boy, Jochi, as his own and never treated him any differently from the other children who were to follow.

Temuchin now had the support of his *anda*, Jamuqa, and his patron, Toghril, and in the wars that followed his spectacular successes began to forge his reputation as a brilliant general and generous leader. Furthermore, a shaman proclaimed that Temuchin had been given a mandate from the Mongol god Tengri (the Eternal Heaven) to rule the steppes and that he had magical powers. Inspired by the legends surrounding the charismatic young chieftain, the Mongolian tribes began to flock to his banner. Unfortunately, Jamuqa became jealous of Temuchin's new status and began to organize those tribes who were scared of Temuchin's rise. In the war that followed, Temuchin and Toghril's alliance faced all the other tribes of the steppes combined. However, the only thing that bound Jamuqa's forces was their fear of Temuchin, and the resulting distrust and lack of cohesive leadership meant that Temuchin was able to overcome and scatter his enemies. The victory also allowed him to settle an old score, and the war culminated with the complete and systematic genocide of the male population of the Tartar tribe. After he had unleashed his fury on them, Temuchin dispersed the female members of the Tartars among the tribes under his command. His tribute to his father was to remove the Tartars from the face of the earth.

Even though he was drenched in the blood of the Tartars, Temuchin showed that his rage was not yet sated and turned his dark gaze on the other score he still had to settle: the tribe who were responsible for his family's exile in the mountains, the Taijut, and in particular their chieftain, who had enticed his father's clan away. After his inevitable victory Temuchin treated them as mercilessly as he had the Tartars.

Further Betrayal

Now that he had avenged the betrayals of his childhood, Temuchin thought that finally his demons had been exorcised. Despite his fame as an invincible warlord, he was happy to remain loyal to Toghril. To solidify their relationship and gain security for his sons, Temuchin approached him to propose a marriage between his son Jochi and one of Toghril's daughters. However, unknown to Temuchin, Jamuqa, his blood brother turned bitter adversary, had fled to Toghril's army after his last defeat and had become good friends with Toghril's son. Bitterly jealous of Temuchin's success, they convinced Toghril that he had been plotting behind his back. And so in 1203 Temuchin discovered that not only was his marriage proposal rejected, but their alliance was over and the vast armies of Toghril were marching to attack him under Jamuqa's command. His mentor had embraced his arch-enemy.

The battle that followed was the worst that Temuchin had experienced. Despite the excellence of his leadership and the heroism of his generals, his army was overwhelmingly outnumbered. He used the cover of darkness to retreat into the hills, and soon the tribes that he had led repeatedly to victory began to desert him and join his enemies. For the third time in his life Temuchin was forced to hide in the mountains, with a dwindling band of followers. They suffered tremendous hardships, but despite his predicament Temuchin understood the fickle loyalties of the steppes, and eventually the alliance against him began to crumble. The following autumn Temuchin was ready to act, and he struck at Toghril's diminished force in a surprise attack. The battle lasted for three days and nights, but finally Toghril fled, only to be caught and killed.

Despite his spectacular victory, against the odds, Temuchin still had to face Jamuqa and his armies in order to decide once and for all who would rule the steppes. However, after his victory in the resulting battle, he discovered that Jamuqa had fled again. Temuchin hunted him for four years across the steppes until Jamuqa's followers, in desperation, handed him over, only to be promptly executed by Temuchin for their disloyalty. Confronted by his childhood friend, Temuchin was moved to compassion and offered to forgive Jamuqa and spare his life. But in a final act of defiance Jamuqa demanded to be executed. Reluctantly Temuchin gave the order, and Jamuqa was trampled to death by horses. Temuchin had finally avenged all those who had betrayed him.

Dawn of the Great Khan

In 1206, at a gathering of all the clans of the steppes, Temuchin, aged thirty-nine, was proclaimed as Genghis Khan, or "Great King," and ruler of "all people who live in felt tents." Despite the horrendous trials of his life, he now stood as the undisputed ruler of a nation of lethal warriors that before his birth had not even existed. Its creation had been the incidental by-product of the endless betrayals he had suffered. But a nation born of such rage could not remain at peace for long. Genghis Khan had created a loaded gun, and sooner or later he would have to find something to point it at.

The Destroyer Creates a Nation

Before he did so, Genghis Khan set about taming the brutal society that had formed him. He was determined that he would never again suffer the agonies of personal betrayal, so he set about changing the culture of shifting allegiances that had plagued the steppes for centuries. It was the inherent social structure of the steppes that led to the chaos and anarchy of which he had been a victim all his life. He was wise enough to know that unless he changed the underlying causes of this, his hard-won position would be short-lived. The four institutions that he created would become the pillars of the new Mongol nation.

Genghis Khan was not too proud to learn from those around him. The Mongols had no written script of their own, so he simply adopted that of the Naiman, the last tribe he had fought in his war against Jamuqa. Once this essential building block was put in place, he then began to develop and implement perhaps the greatest contribution to the new Mongol nation: his list of laws as to how the Mongol state and empire should be governed.

THE YASA

The Yasa was the written record of decrees, laws, and recorded customs that were designed to regulate all aspects of Mongol life. Crimes such as murder, adultery, desertion from military service, robbery, and plunder all became punishable by death, as were merchants who became bankrupt for a third time.

His third major development demonstrated his incredible talent for organization and his understanding of the requirements of effective government.

THE YAM—THE MEDIEVAL PONY EXPRESS

Genghis Khan was aware that unless he knew what was going on in every corner of his growing empire the threat of rebellion was ever present. To solve this problem he created the Yam, a mounted courier service that linked his empire through a series of routes that crisscrossed the country. The Yam was so impressive that Marco Polo commented on it as a feat of organizational wonder. But the one area that truly demonstrated Genghis Khan's brilliance was his development of an organization that would be the zenith of his organizational ability and was breathtaking in its modernity.

THE MONGOL MILITARY MACHINE

When it came to skill with a bow and on horseback the Mongol warriors had no equal. Combined with their extreme toughness developed through their harsh existence on the steppes, this made them natural soldiers, but what they had always lacked was organization and discipline. The first revolutionary thing Genghis Khan did was to break up the tribal allegiances that were a fundamental part of steppe life.

He divided his army into groups of tens, hundreds, and thousands, and distributed the members of different tribes into different military units. Each soldier was encouraged to develop loyalty to the other members of his unit rather than to the tribe they had been born into. Some tribes that had been particularly troublesome in the past were completely dismantled and their men distributed throughout the whole army. Any soldier who attempted to change unit without permission was punished by death. Genghis Khan also introduced a new concept called the *keshig*. This was his personal bodyguard, and by the time he was proclaimed Genghis Khan it had grown to ten thousand men tasked with guarding him at all times and protecting him during battles. Each member of the *keshig* was loyal to Genghis Khan and looked to him, rather than to their old tribal group, for personal advancement. Furthermore, the leaders of the army were picked from its ranks, and through this Genghis Khan ensured his total autocracy throughout his new empire. So effective was his restructuring of the army that soon afterwards the old tribal allegiances faded away and all loyalty was focused on one man, Genghis Khan.

FIGHTING STYLE

The Mongols were natural soldiers and their army consisted solely of horsemen. They had learned riding and archery since they were children and these skills were a part of who they were. Each soldier took up to four spare horses with him while on campaign and even slept on horseback if needed. This was the secret of their ability to cover great distances in incredibly short periods of time. They were also able to endure grinding hardships and survive on the most basic of rations. But it was the modernity of their tactics that was most striking. Medieval fighting consisted of chaotic and enormous pitched battles where opponents would hack at one another until the side with the most men left standing emerged victorious. Knights in armor, although individually brave, were not trained generals and were more interested in personal heroics than in deploying effective cohesive strategies. The Mongols, on the other hand, avoided hand-to-hand fighting as much as they possibly could. Every man in the army fought as part of a group and knew his place exactly in the maneuver that had been practiced constantly during training. From the point at which the enemy was sighted, to the inevitable Mongol victory, their generals would use an intricate system of flags and torch signals to lead their troops through a series of choreographed tactics and annihilate their bewildered opponents with surgical precision.

Once Genghis Khan had created a lethal war machine, he felt ready to use it. The first country to experience the storm of the Mongols was China.

The Invasion of China

The key theme that characterized the campaigns of Genghis Khan was the lack of overriding vision and purpose. Despite his military genius he was still a culturally bereft barbarian at heart. Just like his rise to power in the steppes, his subsequent dominance of Asia came about by accident. His conquering of the world was simply a series of random revenge-takings rather than the result of a grand plan.

It was in this spirit that he began raids into the empire of China. The "invasion" began when the Mongols entered the Chin territory and then, splitting into smaller forces, rode in all directions across the countryside, destroying everything, and killing everyone they found. They would have continued in this way had they not ridden straight into a huge Chin army at Huan-erh-tsui. What should have happened, what had always happened before, was that the steppe horsemen, when confronted with an imperial army, would turn tail and ride back to Mongolia, taking as much booty as they could carry. This time the Chin army were amazed to see the vastly smaller Mongol force ride into perfect battle formation and attack them. Genghis Khan's new model army proved unstoppable. Within hours the lethally efficient horsemen had destroyed the 70,000–strong Chin army. Nine years later a Taoist monk passed by the area on his way to the court of Genghis Khan and reported that the whole area was still littered with human bones.

Following this devastation, the Mongols managed to reach the gates of the Chin capital Chung-tu (modern Beijing), but due to their complete lack of ability in siege warfare they had to turn around and ride back home.

In 1213 they returned and again reached Chung-tu. But again, lacking the necessary knowledge and technology, they retreated from its gates. This time they rode out across the North China plain. There they discovered the vast agricultural population of northern China, and responded in the only way they knew how: by slaughtering tens of thousands of them. They then returned to the gates of Chung-tu, carrying vast amounts of plunder and countless slaves. However, whilst there, a plague swept through their ranks. As he had neither the skill nor the men to take Chung-tu, Genghis Khan was on the point of leaving for Mongolia again when the Chin emperor unexpectedly sued for peace.

For centuries the Chinese empire had endured the periodic raids from the uncultured barbarians who flooded into their lands from the steppes. They had learned to accept this scourge in much the same way that they coped with floods and other natural disasters. However, such was the enduring strength of the Chinese culture that rather than being destroyed by these horsemen, they invariably absorbed and assimilated them. The founders of the Chin dynasty themselves had once been tribal horsemen who, once they settled in northern China, had been tamed by it, and swapped their furs for fine silks. Their usual means of coping with the steppe tribes was to back various tribes against one another and so fight barbarians with barbarians. The second method was simply to buy them off. They knew that all the tribesmen wanted was booty, and calculated that it was cheaper in the long run to bribe them rather than fight with them. This was exactly what they decided to do when Genghis Khan's army was camped outside their city. However, this time the two parties had perceived the outcome in profoundly different ways. The Chin emperor had given Genghis Khan one of his daughters to add to his ever-increasing number of wives. As a result, Genghis Khan thought that the emperor, seeing his invincible power, had accepted him as the dominant monarch in the region and was content to rule over a subservient kingdom in return for being allowed to live. But the idea of accepting an illiterate barbarian as his overlord was as unthinkable to a Chin emperor as building a city was to Genghis Khan. This simple misconception would cost the Chin dynasty their very existence.

While Genghis Khan was back in his tent, surrounded by his new wealth, his wives, and the cult-like adoration of his invincible soldiers, the Chin emperor was giving serious thought to his court's proximity to his Mongolian neighbors from hell. He realized to his deep discomfort that Chung-tu was too close geographically to the northern passes to Mongolia, and so he took the perfectly sensible step of relocating his court to K'ai-feng, south of the Yellow River. By doing this, he had unwittingly awoken Genghis Khan's childhood demon. For when Genghis Khan heard the news, he perceived that by moving his court, the Chin emperor had shown that he did not trust the lord of the Mongols. In a felt tent far away on a Mongolian plain, Genghis Khan uttered the word "Betrayal."

And so in 1214 the Mongols returned again to Chung-tu, but this time Genghis Khan did not have money on his mind. He had come for revenge, and he was ready to stay until he got it. The citizens were distraught. They had been abandoned by their emperor and knew their fate once the Mongolians took their city. They resisted as best they could and resorted to eating the corpses of their dead, tortured by the knowledge that the longer they held out, the worse their fate would be. In the summer of 1215 the city fell.

Chung-tu was one of the leading cities in China. It was a rich commercial and culture center with beautiful parks, palaces, and museums. All of these were destroyed by the Mongols. The sack lasted more than a month and was methodical in its madness. Mongol horsemen rode in formation through the streets, firing lighted arrows into the wooden houses, and reduced the whole city to a blackened wreck. After their work was done the roads were paved with battered bodies and the ground was greasy with human fat. By one of the walls was a huge pile of bones said to be those of over 60,000 girls who had thrown themselves from the ramparts rather than fall into the hands of the Mongols. News of the destruction raced through the kingdoms of Asia, and all of China resounded with the implications. Under their new leader, the previously disorganized horsemen of the steppes were now capable of destroying cities. This had never happened before. A new, dark, and bloody age had dawned.

The Mongols showed not the slightest interest in colonizing the lands they had conquered so easily. It was conceptual anathema to them. Despite his hellish talent for bringing death and destruction to his enemies, Genghis Khan's ignorance of the workings of sedentary societies meant that he had no idea what to do with a territory once he had conquered it. (He seriously considered "depopulating" the whole of northern China to provide pastures for his horses until a desperate Chinese administrator convinced him that live peasants paid more taxes than dead ones!) As a result, the Chin were not defeated for a further twenty years, a job Genghis Khan would bequeath to his sons. Once his need for revenge had been sated in China, he characteristically lost interest in the campaign and returned to Mongolia to turn his attention elsewhere.

Khwarazm Shah

To the west of Mongolia lay the Islamic empire of the Khwarazm Shah, Sultan Muhammad II. This empire, now modern Uzbekistan, had a huge army made up of Turkish mercenaries. While Genghis Khan had been carving out his empire, the Khwarazm Shah had expansionist aspirations of his own. He had already pushed south into Persian territory, and in 1210 he conquered the kingdom of Transoxania, which included the magical cities of Bukhara and Samarkand. Unfortunately the Khwarazm Shah was a somewhat misguided individual. He referred to himself as the "Shadow of God on Earth" and "the chosen Prince of Allah," and even claimed that he was the new Alexander the Great. Encouraged by his initial successes, he had begun to plan the invasion of China. It was at this time that he heard about the new power that had arisen in Mongolia. One of his ambassadors had been present at the sacking of Chung-tu and had returned with horrific tales of the military brilliance and excessive brutality of the Mongols.

After the fall of Chung-tu, the Khwarazm Shah sent an envoy to Genghis Khan to establish a relationship between the two empires. The Mongols believed that the safety of ambassadors was sacred and Genghis Khan treated the envoy with the utmost courtesy, sending him home with the news that Genghis Khan viewed himself as the ruler of the East and that the Khwarazm Shah was the ruler of the West. He was assured that Genghis Khan wanted peace between the two neighbors and wished to open trade relations between them. But when in 1218, in accordance with their agreement, 450 Mongol merchants, along with a Mongol ambassador, arrived at Utrar on the frontiers of his kingdom, the Khwarazm Shah had them all arrested and later executed on the pretext that they were spies. Despite his rage, Genghis Khan sent another three diplomats to demand that the Khwarazm Shah make amends in an attempt to avoid war. But as if he was on a trajectory to destruction, the Khwarazm Shah had their leader executed and burned the beards of the other two Mongol ambassadors.

Perhaps the Khwarazm Shah believed that he was invincible and that this uncouth barbarian would soon be taught a lesson; perhaps he genuinely believed that he was "the chosen Prince of Allah." But with this final murder, he not only signed his own death warrant, but single-handedly brought about the greatest catastrophe ever to descend upon the Islamic world, a catastrophe so complete that to this day many of the areas it touched have still not recovered.

Preparation for War

All across the steppes, men were summoned to leave their herds and make their way to join the Mongol army. Genghis Khan raised a force of 200,000 men, the largest Mongol army ever assembled, but despite this, he was acutely aware that it was less than half the size of that of the Khwarazm Shah. He decided to call on a previous agreement with the king of the neighboring Tanguts, who, as his vassal, had agreed to send him troops if requested. However, Genghis Khan was shocked when the Tangut king replied that if he could not raise enough troops himself, then he had no right to call himself Great Khan. Genghis Khan was enraged by this response, but was in no position at this point to do anything about it.

The army was split into four divisions, the first commanded by Genghis Khan himself, and the others by his sons and generals. The first three divisions marched towards the Khwarazm Shah's borders in order to engage and distract him. Meanwhile, Genghis Khan, under a cloak of secrecy, led his division quietly out of Mongolia, into Transoxania, and then simply disappeared. It was as if they had ridden off the edge of the world. He was in fact leading his entire force on a secret route through the Kyzyl Kum desert—a barren, inhospitable terrain that was generally believed to be impenetrable. While the forces of the Khwarazm Shah were preoccupied with the divisions attacking their borders, a Mongol army under the command of its most lethal general was creeping up on them—and they did not even know that it existed. Six months later the unimaginable happened. The citizens of Bukhara awoke to find a Mongol army camped outside their walls. Genghis Khan had appeared out of nowhere, 400 miles inside their country. Paralyzed by abject terror, the soldiers defending the city decided to abandon it and make their escape, but the citizens watched from the walls as the Mongols annihilated them effortlessly. A contemporary Persian writer recorded that after the slaughter it looked as if the plain "was a tray filled with blood."

Psychological Warfare—The Wrath of God

The despairing citizens of Bukhara surrendered immediately and let their worst nightmare ride unopposed into the city. Genghis Khan made straight for the mosque, thinking that it was the Sultan's palace. After it was explained to him that it was their most sacred shrine, he had it converted into stables. The Korans were burned and hay was kept in their sacred cases. As the inhabitants shivered in terror, the prophet of doom began his own sermon. Mounting the pulpit, he addressed their deepest fears: "I am the wrath of God. Had you not committed great sins, he would not have sent me to punish you." In the minds of the deeply religious Muslim community, it appeared as if their God had deserted them.

The repercussions of Genghis Khan's victory then unfolded with a terrible predictability. There followed the usual slaughter and a rounding-up of slaves, but the majority of the population were allowed to leave with only the clothes they were wearing. However, rather than an act of clemency on the part of the avenging Khan, this was all a part of his master plan. As they flooded into the surrounding country-side, leaving their city to be destroyed behind them, they spread the news of the fate of Bukhara, terrorizing the inhabitants with their stories of the Mongol hordes who had appeared at their gates as if by some black art, and describing the fate of all those who opposed them. The hysteria culminated at the gates of Samarkand, the Khwarazm Shah's capital, exactly as Genghis Khan had planned it. As the

Mongols approached the capital they drove prisoners from Bukhara who had been press-ganged into their army before them. Their choice was simple: either join the Mongols and fight their own countrymen, or be executed on the spot. As the despairing captives marched to their doom, the defenders of Samarkand had no choice but to shower them with arrows. Their screams, combined with the tales of utter horror that had already infested the city, destroyed any fighting spirit Samarkand might have had. Before even setting eyes on the city, Genghis Khan had killed its spirit. Samarkand, the Jewel of Islam, which could easily have held out for a year, surrendered after only five days.

Despite the total destruction of the major cities, both the Khwarazm Shah and his son, Jalal al-Din, escaped. True to his nature, Genghis Khan pursued them relentlessly. Eventually they led him to the banks of the River Indus in Pakistan, and his brilliant general, Subodai, into the heart of Russia, where he annihilated every European army he encountered. Years later, when they returned to expand the Mongol empire, Subodai's armies would reach as far as the walls of Vienna, and only the death of Genghis's successor, Ogedei, saved western Europe from complete destruction. Their route is scattered with once magnificent cities and cultures that to this day stand as broken, silent witnesses to the excesses of Genghis Khan's rage.

Final Days, Final Revenge

On the banks of the River Indus, Genghis Khan received the news that the Khwarazm Shah was dead. His need for revenge satisfied, he simply stopped and prepared to go home to Mongolia. In 1225, almost five years later, his army finally arrived home. He was now sixty, but even in his advanced years he still had one final betrayal to avenge. He was determined to punish the king of the Tanguts for his refusal to help him fight the Khwarazm. However, shortly after the start of the campaign, he suffered a bad fall from his horse while hunting and suffered serious internal injuries. Despite the pleas of his doctors, he refused to call off the campaign until the Tanguts had been defeated. In 1227 Genghis Khan died as his armies burst into the city. Upon hearing the news that their leader, the Great Khan, the founder of the Mongol nation, the accidental conqueror of the world, was dead, the Mongol horde went berserk and killed every living thing within the city in memory of him.

SECTION TWO: LESSONS
DRIVEN BY DEMONS—WHAT WE CAN LEARN FROM
GENGHIS KHAN

The Motivational Methods of Alexander the Great vs. Genghis Khan's

We may not like to admit it, but in many ways Genghis Khan can teach us a lot more about motivation than Alexander the Great. Why? He came from nothing, did not have the advantage of a successful father to emulate, could not read or write and so had no romantic literature or philosophies to draw upon, and he most definitely did not have an intellectual giant as a teacher. In fact, he did not have any education at all. Yet in his lifetime he overcame insurmountable odds and created an empire four times the size of that of Alexander. If Alexander was consumed with his vision, Genghis Khan was consumed with his rage. Alexander would have considered Genghis Khan an uncouth barbarian and Genghis Khan would probably have thought that Alexander was a pampered prince born into privilege. Alexander founded the "West"; Genghis Khan nearly annihilated it. They could not have been more different, yet they both achieved identical goals: the domination of their known worlds. But it is not only in their backgrounds that they were the opposites of one another. Close study of their lives from a motivational psychology point of view reveals that despite the appearance of their sharing the same urge to conquer, their motives sprang from opposite sides of the spectrum. They both achieved the same goal, but for diametrically opposed reasons. The impact this has on our understanding of ourselves and what drives us is immeasurable.

"Must" Is the Ultimate Motivator

To understand this, then, we have to look at what actually drives us as human beings. When we are in the throes of excitement while pursuing a goal, or battling with our apathy and sloth when we can't seem to be bothered to do anything, it can sometimes feel as if our motivations are random affairs that have no rhyme or reason, but this is not the case. All our motivations are created by the same internal and external factors consistently, and once we understand what they are and the effect they have on us we can begin to pull our own strings rather than feel we are at their mercy. So let's begin by looking at "Maslow's Hierarchy of Needs."

Psychologist Abraham Maslow professed that a human being's needs were arranged in a hierarchy. It looks like this:

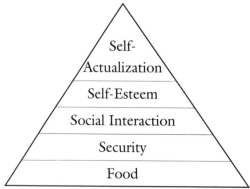

His theory states that humans have needs that have to be

fulfilled on each level before they can progress on to the next. The most basic need is to eat. If human beings are hungry, they will think of nothing else until they have eaten. Once the meal is over, they have to start looking for food all over again. Simply surviving takes up all their time. Once that need is fulfilled, we then begin to think of shelter from the elements, our self-preservation and security from attackers. Once these two basic needs have been satisfied, then we begin to crave acceptance and interaction with other humans. Once we have friends and a social network, we begin to think of our self-esteem and our position within that group. And finally, if we are lucky enough to have a reliable source of food, a secure, sheltered home and the acceptance of a social group around us, we begin to think of our highest human need: that of expressing ourselves creatively, learning and discovering who we are. So basically, Maslow said that if a human is starving, freezing, and being attacked, then the last thing on their mind is making friends and learning Spanish. It goes without saying that the strongest drives are the bottom two basic needs. From my own personal experience, I know that if you are hungry and freezing to death, motivating yourself is not a problem. The reason why the increase in quality of life in the developed world has been exponential in recent human history is because for millennia mankind had been struggling just to have enough to eat. Once they had developed the technology and agriculture to provide a surplus of food, with their shelter and security needs met in settled communities, they could begin to turn their attention to developing higher cultural expressions and more advanced technologies because they had free time on their hands.

The reason that I introduced Maslow's theory is because it gives us an even deeper insight into the motivational forces that drive us, and the opposing forms of motivation that Alexander the Great and Genghis Khan represented.

Alexander's motivation was based on the fifth level. He was on a quest to fulfill his intellectual and spiritual needs, in the most complete way, by discovering the ends of the earth, creating one world, and his personal deification. This form of motivation is usually the weakest, as failing to earn a PhD or paint a masterpiece (although possibly bitterly disappointing), is rarely life-threatening. Genghis Khan, on the other hand, spent his early life struggling to fulfill the first levels— food and shelter—and was haunted all his life by lack of security in the shape of the threat of betrayal and attack. He was never trying to express or fulfill his dreams as Alexander was; Genghis Khan was simply trying to survive the only way he knew how, with the limited options available to him.

That is the problem that all of us who wish we were more motivated suffer from. In our culture, our needs are usually based in the realms of self-actualization, or "fifth-level goals," as I call them. To put it simply, we are too comfortable to strive. In most cases, if we don't succeed, it doesn't really matter; our inaction won't kill us, we can just switch on the TV instead. I am very wary of excessive comfort. It makes me intellectually, emotionally, and spiritually "fat." Excessive comfort is very bad for you and can drain you of all your motivation. That is why people with Alexander the Great's drive are so rare in our comfortable society. However, once you have finished this chapter you will know how to remedy this.

So how can we, who live in such a pampered society, tap

into that ferocious motivating power that Genghis Khan displayed, and use it to our advantage? Before we learn how, we have to look at another fundamental aspect of what drives us, the terrible twins, Pain and Pleasure.

Internal vs. External Motivation

Every human action can be distilled down to two basic drives: the desire for pleasure, and the avoidance of pain. It is these basic drives that have guaranteed the survival of the human race. By rewarding our early ancestors with pain or pleasure, these physical and emotional stimuli ensured that they continued to eat, mate, and avoid anything that led to physical pain, be it confronting wild animals or eating poisonous fruit, all without them even having to think about it.

That the stimuli of simple pain and pleasure are extremely effective is obvious. Our present existence is evidence of that. However, what many of us do not realize is that, despite the huge differences in our physical environments, we are physically the same today as our ancestors who lived thousands of years ago (in a very basic sense). Despite the fact that most of us in the developed world have an abundance of food and very comfortable lives, we are still driven by the avoidance of pain and the desire for pleasure. "That's obvious," you may say, but do you realize that your failure or success in the pursuit of your goals is also attributable to those basic two drives that ensured the survival of our early ancestors?

In the last chapter we looked at how we must understand what our goals mean to us, what they represent. The reason that this is so important is because once we understand the reason behind why we want the new house, promotion, or fancy car, we can see the profound truth behind what evolutionary force is actually driving us. We can gain an insight into whether we are being motivated by the avoidance of pain or the desire for pleasure.

Let's use the desire to solve money problems as an example, since it's something that most of us can relate to. Imagine that you wanted to become financially independent. Now ask yourself: "Why do I want to achieve this goal?" Is it because . . .

- I want to be rich; *or*
- I don't want to be poor?

If you are going on a diet, is it because . . .

- I want to be slim; *or*
- I don't want to be fat?

This may seem like semantics, but understanding how we motivate ourselves is very important, and in each case the emotions driving our responses are profoundly different. The first answer in each case is driven by the motivation discussed in the lessons from Alexander, while the second answers are motivated primarily by fear or discomfort. In the first answers you are moving towards an ideal vision; in the second you are moving away from a threatening feeling. Believe it or not, the greatest driving force in evolution and human nature is the fear and threat of pain. For years I used to listen to motivational speakers going on about how we had to visualize positive goals and have bright images in our minds of how we want to be. This is true and very helpful; however, in the real world, when I began to build my first business, I found that the times I was most motivated, in fact the times when there was literally nothing else on my mind, were when I was just getting started and was scared of going bust. They were pretty stressful times but the creativity and drive that the fear unleashed was incredible and it got things done.

Here's a more graphic example. While on my expedition to K2 I was wearing a pair of high-altitude boots designed by NASA that keep my feet safe to temperatures of minus fifty degrees. As I was climbing over the ridge of a glacier my boot burst through some ice and my leg plunged into ice-cold water up to my thigh. The water poured in over the top of the gaiter and in an instant my foot and socks were soaked. As I clambered out I heard the other climbers whispering frantically in French and in the moonlight saw the look on their faces. I did not need them to tell me: the water would soon freeze around my foot, rapidly accelerating frostbite, and in the sub-zero temperatures it was almost certain I would lose my foot. I had one chance. If I could reach the next camp, further up the mountain, get into the tent, take off the boot and get into my sleeping bag, then I might be OK. I broke the land speed record that night. Despite the altitude, the hazards, and the weight of my pack, I took off like a rocket and climbed the distance in less than half the time it would otherwise have taken. All the positive images of the beauty of the views or being the first to the top could never have driven me as powerfully as the terror of amputation. Fear works, and by the end of this chapter you will know how to use it creatively to your advantage.

Harness the Power of Your Greatest Ally

When the student is ready, the teacher appears.

Ancient Chinese Proverb

Our fears are the unsung heroes of our lives, our greatest friends and allies. Unfortunately, very few of us realize this, as the sensation of fear is so unpleasant. However, this sensation masks the three gifts that our fears offer us:

OUR FEARS REVEAL WHO WE THINK WE ARE

In chapter one we discussed the importance of our self-image and our inner perception of the world as the single greatest determinant of our experience of life. However, our self-image is sometimes hard for us to see, as we are so used to being who we are. Nothing reveals our self-imposed limitations better than our fears. Our fears are deeply personal, and what terrifies one person may not even raise the pulse of another. In that way your fear is a highly sensitive emotional barometer and is a useful tool for exploring the perceptions that form your world. Thankfully most of the fear responses that we experience today in our culture are not triggered by truly threatening situations such as the threat of physical harm. Rather mostly we fear imaginary demons such as failure, ridicule, or job interviews. In these non-threatening situations we can use that fear as a mirror to accurately reflect how we see ourselves. Next time you want to do something but feel scared, rather than backing off, listen to what your fear is telling you about what you believe about yourself and the situation. Rather than taking your fear as an absolute truth, look at it as an indicator of the thoughts that dictate your life. Here's an example. If you are gripped by fear at the thought of a job interview, then what is that fear telling you? Could it be that you don't believe you are a good communicator, intelligent, or qualified enough? The fear could mean any number of things, but none of them are necessarily true. In many cases your fears are caused by your subjective impression of yourself and the situation, not the reality.

As our fears contract, our life expands

Unless you confront your fear and go through it, that fear will keep you exactly where you are for the rest of your life. And that is the second gift that fear offers us, the gift that we often fail to see when we are in its grip: that in the same way that pushing yourself physically through exercise makes you stronger, pushing through your fears expands the possibilities of what you are capable of and rewards you with a wider and fuller life. This is what Ralph Waldo Emerson meant when he revealed, "Do the thing and you will have its power." Many of us spend our whole lives trying to avoid fear, but in essence what we are avoiding is life. Run from your fears and you run from a richer life. Face them and a whole new world opens up to you. This is always easier said than done, but the self-respect and sense of possibility that conquering a fear bestows upon us is one of the most liberating feelings we can experience.

Fear gives you instant motivation

Whether we like it or not, fear is the greatest motivator available to humanity. It is an evolutionary tool designed to keep us alive and to get us away from serious trouble without having to think about it too much. If you have a gang chasing you with baseball bats you do not have to ask yourself if running is aligned with your highest aspirations and values.

So let's meet some of our motivational new best friends:

- Humiliation
- The fear of rejection
- Global ridicule
- Bankruptcy
- Dying alone, cold, and hungry

OK, I may sound as if I am being glib, but I am deadly serious. Don't believe me? Let's use the weight-loss example again. Incidentally, the reason weight loss is such a good example in motivation is because it is not dependent upon any special talent or market trend, and is something that we as individuals have complete control over. Unless you have a medical condition, being overweight is entirely a function of your own behavior, and let's face it, when it comes to being overweight, the only medical condition that most of suffer from is "cake retention."

Back to the example. I am going to let you in on a secret as to what my next business is going to be. I am going to become the world's greatest weight-loss guru, and I GUARANTEE rapid results! This is how it will work. When a seven-hundred-pound client comes to me and laments that he just can't get motivated to lose weight, I will take out a gun, put it in his mouth, and whisper, "I am going to visit you in a month, and if you haven't lost twenty-five pounds by then, I am going to blow your brains out." I guarantee you that for once he will have motivation, rather than doughnuts, coming out of his ears. Of course this method is dependent on two things: him believing I will do it; the police not catching me until he has reached his dream weight. If he is willing to pay for the deluxe package, then I will also threaten to shoot his whole family. Of course his fee would include the cost of the extra bullets and my dry-cleaning bill. But trust me, he *would* lose weight. Now, what point am I trying to make with this sick joke?

The reason that so many people have so much trouble getting motivated is because *they have absolutely no fear of the consequences of not being motivated.* The consequences of doing nothing do not scare them, and as a result they do . . . nothing, except moan that they can't get motivated.

How many times have you seen this in films? The loving father is trundling along with his life when suddenly some gangsters kidnap his wife and children and demand a huge ransom. In an instant his every waking thought is obsessed with getting his family back and doing everything in his power to raise the money. How ridiculous and implausible would it be if when the kidnapper called and demanded the money the father replied, "Well, I don't really have the confidence and I am not very good under pressure. I also have a lot going on right now and . . ." Exactly. But if you'd asked him a week earlier if he was going to go for a promotion to earn more money, he might have come out with those very same excuses. The fear transforms him in an instant.

I do not believe there is such a thing as an unmotivated person. By that I mean somebody who is simply incapable of being motivated. The reason the person is unmotivated is because the reward of pleasure and the threat of pain are not real to them. When somebody says, "Work hard and you will get promoted," they either believe they are not capable and so will not get the reward, or deep down they actually don't want the reward and so a promotion does not equal pleasure to them. Similarly if you say to the same person, "Lose weight or you will get heart disease," they may accept that intellectually, but the threat will seem so far off that it will have no emotional impact. That is why if you want to maintain high levels of motivation you must use your imagination to make the reward or threat real to you.

Use Your Imagination to Make the Reward or Threat Real to You

So many times when I am asked to advise people on what to do in their businesses or how to motivate themselves they say to me, "Yeah, I already know that." Or "Yeah, I know I should do that." My answer to them is simple: "Really, well why haven't you done it then?" I usually get blank stares after that. But we are all the same. In many instances we know how to do the things that we need to do in order to create a better life for ourselves, get a better job, or lose weight. Loads of us have fitness videos and contraptions, but we are still overweight and wish we were slimmer. The reason is simple:

To know and not to do . . . is not to know.

Read that line again slowly until it sinks in. If you know something but you still can't bring yourself to act on it, even though not acting causes you discomfort, it is because you don't really know it. The penny hasn't quite dropped, and the reason for that is to know something intellectually is not always to know it emotionally.

To know something intellectually is not always to know it emotionally.

It is when we grasp emotionally, why we want to get a promotion, or lose weight, or whatever it is, that we have our "eureka" moment. We finally get it. Unfortunately this moment sometimes only occurs when our lives present us with what Alcoholics Anonymous calls "hitting rock bottom." The moment—and it is totally different for each of us—when the momentum in your life takes you to a point so low that you snap and decide to change. Here are some examples. Let's continue with the weight example. Imagine you are overweight and your partner runs away with a slimmer version of you. Now the difference in weight could be totally irrelevant, but if you believe that it happened because you are overweight then this would trigger deeply unpleasant emotions. At that point you finally know emotionally that you need to lose weight, because when you think of being overweight your brain remembers (remember, we talked about the power of our memories in the last chapter) the humiliation and indignation, and screams, "PAIN!" And what does any living organism do when it feels pain? It does everything in its power to avoid it. Weight loss suddenly becomes a lot easier. (For the record, I don't think there is anything necessarily wrong with being overweight, as long as it doesn't damage your health. But if it makes you miserable then it is a problem.) The same transformative anguish occurs in the father who is made redundant for the third time. Seeing that his kids have no presents at Christmas suddenly motivates him to set up his own business and never work for a big company again.

The event is irrelevant, but what makes the difference is if it causes enough emotional pain. Genghis Khan had numerous "rock bottom" moments in his life: being abandoned once as a child, and twice with his followers when Toghril and Jamuqa turned on him. When we add to that the repeated betrayals he endured, we can see how he was driven throughout his whole life to try and escape and so prevent the pain of abandonment and betrayal hurting him again. In his early life betrayal meant potential death, but even later, when he had a whole army behind him, his greatest motivation to act was still when he felt betrayed.

We have all had painful experiences in our lives, and despite the power of pain in motivating us I would not wish it on anybody. However, the fact remains that the threat of pain is a far greater force in transforming people than the desire for pleasure. The exciting thing is that now that we understand this power and the effect it has on our behavior, we can turn it to our advantage. Rather than waiting for events in life to scare you, you can create rock bottom in your imagination and make it painful.

Create Rock Bottom in Your Imagination . . . and Make It Painful!

Have you ever had six months to study for an exam and left it to the night before? The stress is horrible but your focus is incredible. You always promise that next time you will start in plenty of time, but the following year, there you are again the night before, surrounded with books, cramming like a maniac. Maybe you've never done this, but you will have had your equivalent of it. One of the things that can most effectively erode our self-esteem is really wanting to do something that we know we should do, but just not being able to motivate ourselves to do it. No matter how much we scream at ourselves or give ourselves little pep talks, we still don't do it, and we end up feeling as if we have zero self-discipline, which inevitably damages our self-respect. As we discussed in chapter one, in some instances this inaction can be linked to our values, such as not feeling worthy of achieving the goal, but in most cases the reason for the inaction is a lot simpler. In the example of not studying, six months before the exam the fear of failing is an intellectual awareness not an emotional one; the night before, however, the fear has transformed itself into real emotion. In other words, the threat of pain has become real.

So how do we use this knowledge to our advantage? We do something I call the "Scrooge technique." Even if you haven't read Charles Dickens's *A Christmas Carol*, you must have seen it on TV at Christmas time. If you recall, the miserable miser Scrooge is visited in a dream on Christmas Eve by three ghosts (the ghosts of Christmas Past, Present, and Future). The first two show him his past and present, forcing him to review the implications of his behavior. But it is the third ghost that has the greatest impact. Already chastened by the visions presented by the first two visitors, Scrooge is taken on a journey by the Ghost of Christmas Future, a terrifying specter in a shroud, and shown where his current behavior is leading him. He is shown his own personal "rock bottom." He is utterly terrified, and when he wakes up and finds he is still alive he is completely transformed into a benevolent and kind-hearted philanthropist.

Now let me ask you a question. Where did the spectral journeys take place?

In his imagination.

What, therefore, completely transformed him?

His imagination.

That is the answer to our own lack of motivation. Quite simply, to make the painful implications of our inaction so real to us that our pain/pleasure instincts kick in and drive us away from the inaction that is hurting us.

Let's continue with the example of not studying.

Sit back and imagine yourself opening the exam envelope and getting an "F." Try and imagine how bad this makes you feel, then make it worse. Your friends are laughing at you, your parents are crying, you can't get a job . . . Really lay it on thick and do a Scrooge on yourself. Once you awaken, revel in the fact that you still have six months left and let the relief and gratitude wash over you.

This exercise relies on you feeling very uncomfortable. The negative feelings of getting an "F" have to hurt. If they don't, it won't work. Your imagination is a very powerful thing, so use it to create the same urgency that you would feel if you only had a week left. Make the implications of inaction real to you without going through the pain in reality.

This is an extremely powerful motivator if you really communicate the negative visions to yourself. You can use it to get fit, work harder at your job, anything. The point is not to criticize or chastise yourself but rather to create the pain in an environment that you can control rather than experiencing it in your life and having to get yourself out of a situation you could have avoided. Remember, the pain has to cause you discomfort and feel real to you. If it doesn't, then your mind will just rationalize it and you'll go back to watching TV instead of studying. It is imperative that you really grasp the implications of your current behavior in the same way that Scrooge did and so impel yourself to change it.

External Motivation Is Short Term and Lacks Vision

The motivation inspired by fear and the desire to escape a perceived threat is incredibly powerful, but has equally powerful limitations. The first limitation is that once the threat of pain is removed, the motivation to move away from it evaporates too. If you are no longer being chased then there is no point running. The life of Genghis Khan illustrates this perfectly: once he had defeated the Khwarazm Shah he simply stopped and went home. The threat had gone and with it his ferocious motivation. He had no desire to explore the countries he had encountered or to build cities as Alexander did. This behavior makes Genghis Khan a classic example of threat-driven external motivation. Here is a contemporary example. Imagine a person is motivated to change jobs. If they are motivated internally, as Alexander the Great was, then it could be because they want to earn more, learn more, and grow professionally so that they can move towards their predetermined internal vision of their ideal job. However, if they are motivated by external pain, as Genghis Khan was, then they may have been happy in their job for years until a new manager starts making their life a misery. They have no great career ambition; their motivation is simply to remove the pain that the new manager has created. Interestingly, if their manager suddenly started being nice to them their motivation would evaporate. The pain would have been removed.

The second limitation is that external motivation places the power outside you and lacks direction and vision. It lacks its own destination and simply moves away from the threat that creates it. It is a bit like running as fast as you can whilst looking over your shoulder, or jumping in a taxi and saying to the driver, "Take me anywhere as long as it is away from here." You are more interested in what you are running away from than in where you are going. As in the example above, an externally motivated person is happy once the pain is removed, regardless of where they end up. As a result a person motivated purely by external pain tends only to respond when they are pushed and as a result tends not to be in control of where their life is going.

Now that we understand the profound differences between the internal motivation demonstrated by Alexander the Great and the external motivation demonstrated by Genghis Khan, how can we use this knowledge to transform the way in which we pursue our goals? We can harness the vision of the Macedonian; the drive of the Mongolian.

The Vision of the Macedonian; the Drive of the Mongolian

The combined lesson that Alexander and Genghis Khan teach us is that if you want to lead a fulfilled life with meaningful goals then you must have the compelling vision of Alexander the Great backed up by the driving force of Genghis Khan.

This is a more enlightened and eloquent understanding of what is meant by "the carrot and the stick." Now we understand that internal motivation is creative and vision-led but is easier to give up on, whereas external motivation is threat-driven and incredibly powerful but has no destination and stops once the threat is removed. We can now use this knowledge to bring guidance and power to our motivation in a way that was not possible before. We can pick our goals based on the processes outlined in chapter one; they can inspire us, fulfill us and bring meaning to our lives, and this vision can pull us towards them. However, once we have identified our goals, we can use our imaginations to impress upon ourselves the implications of what will happen to us if we fail and use that artificially created fear to propel us towards them. The more powerfully we engage our imaginations to create both these sensations, the more unstoppable we will be. We can be inspired by the vision of Alexander to expand our horizons and dare to see a life for ourselves that previously we would never have believed possible. This vision can inspire us to go to night classes or the gym when we are tired after a hard day's work, but when we feel that it is too difficult and want to give up we can use our primal fear response to keep us on track and remove giving up as an option.

Now that we have studied the motivational lessons from Genghis Khan's life, let's have a look at some of the other invaluable lessons that we can learn from him.

Restricted Options = Restricted Outcomes

The reason I stressed the importance of quality mentors, role models, and peer groups in chapter one is because they provide us with an essential asset that we need in our lives: choices. In evolutionary terms, the more choices or options a species has, the more likely it is to survive. Once a person is motivated to do something, especially if it is to escape from an external threat, the more options they have at their disposal, the more likely they are to succeed, or in more extreme instances survive. In the case of Genghis Khan, he was an illiterate barbarian, despite his military genius. When he was threatened and forced to respond, as at so many times in his life, he could only do so using the limited means at his disposal. His only options were to run or fight. He literally did not know anything else. Of course life in the medieval steppes was by its very nature restricted, but the lesson is the same nonetheless and can give us an insight into the implications of having limited options and choices in a modern setting.

As we discussed in chapter one, our motivation to achieve a goal takes place within the context of who we are in terms of our peer group, values, etc. Once a person becomes motivated to do something, their mind auto-matically starts looking for a way to achieve it. They start looking at their options. This is a positive process if the person has been brought up in an environment that contributes positive solutions, but that is not always the case. In America, for example, many people have accepted the cultural vision of the American dream. However, the options open to a Harvard graduate and those available to a person brought up in a deprived inner-city ghetto are profoundly different. Many of the world's most famous gangsters were highly intelligent, motivated, and determined individuals who simply did not have quality options open to them and so channeled their energies into criminal activities.

If we want to achieve our goals in life then we will find the journey a lot easier if we endeavor to expand the behavioral choices available to us. Our options will determine whether our motivation takes us in a direction we want to go or one that compromises our lives and leads us into trouble. Here's an example. Imagine that you have been sacked unfairly by a boss who treated you like an idiot. You go home enraged and are highly motivated to get your own back. At this point your mind will start scanning your options and the answer it gives you will be a product of everything we have discussed so far. If you have developed contacts, worked on your self-image, and done a good job to date, you will be able to come up with a couple of positive ways of getting revenge. Here are two examples:

- Get a job with a competitor and do so well that your ex-boss is referred to as the guy who forced you to leave.

   Or my personal favorite, you might

- Use your rage to build your own competing business, buy your old company and sack him.

However, if you have not developed a whole series of good options in your life, you might channel your anger into waiting for him in the car park, beating him up, and trashing his company car. This would not only land you in jail but also prove him right and render you unemployable.

   Both responses are products of high levels of motivation, but the options you have developed or will develop determine where that motivation will take you. In some cases a highly motivated person with restricted options is a very dangerous thing. However, it is not as dangerous as a highly successful person who has not grasped the fact that power without sophistication is perilous.

Power Without Sophistication Is Dangerous

Let me tell you something that happens a lot in business circles. A guy makes a lot of money and turns up the next day in a car the size of a bus, dressed head to toe in designer clothes that don't match, covered in tacky jewelry, with his wife on his arm looking like Dolly Parton on a bad day. They have had the makeover from hell. It cracks me up that some people have a desperate need to proclaim their wealth to the world but all they demonstrate is that they have lots of money and no taste. Why am I telling you this? The above example, despite being tacky, is totally harmless, but in many other cases the wielding of financial power without sophistication is anything but. Once a person succeeds in a given arena, be it sport, music, or business, the world seems automatically to believe that they are brilliant in other areas too. More disturbingly, they themselves seem to think that their success in one field means that their opinions on a whole range of diverse subjects are suddenly worthy of a public platform.

One thing that has struck me when I have met people who have succeeded on a huge scale is that often their beliefs in areas such as religion or politics have not evolved since they were much younger. Being able to use your success to promote what you believe in is a very important right. So when we begin to succeed materially it is essential that we also endeavor to grow in the other areas of our lives, rather than simply being brilliant at one limited thing. Unless we do so, can we really call ourselves successful? The Mongol hordes demonstrated the terrifying consequences of extreme power placed in the hands of unsophisticated people. Their military brilliance was not matched by cultural brilliance. Having conquered huge territories, they knew nothing better than to slaughter the inhabitants. They were not sadists; they simply did not know any other way. As we begin to succeed in life, it is essential that we endeavor to increase our compassion, humility, and wisdom and not just our bank balance.

However, despite his brutality, one of the things that I admire about Genghis Khan was that he had the humility and confidence to see his limitations. He knew that, despite his genius, he was still an illiterate tribesman. Even more impressive was the fact that he did not let that hold him back. He knew that to succeed, you must surround yourself with talented people.

Gather Talented People Around You

There is a story I love about Henry Ford that sums up perfectly the attitude of people who build successful teams and businesses. A journalist was mocking him relentlessly in the press, pointing out that he had not had a formal education and as a result had very poor general knowledge. Eventually they confronted one another and the journalist tried to exploit the meeting to make a fool out of the founder of the Ford Motor Company. He began to fire question after question at him, none of which Ford knew the answers to. Finally, after the last question, Ford said in exasperation, "I don't know, but give me five minutes and I'll find a man who does."

In one line Henry Ford had summed up the essential trait necessary if you want to build a business empire: the ability to find and harness the talents of people who have knowledge and skills in the areas that you don't. People can get so hung up on getting straight As and the right degree. Doing well in exams is important and education is essential in order to appreciate the wonder of the world that we live in and get the most out of it, but the skills necessary to achieve in life are more elusive than those found in textbooks. We are often led to believe that if we study hard in school it will provide us with a successful life, but this is quite simply not the case. Here is another little anecdote that demonstrates this point. Two businessmen are sitting watching a game show where the contestants are tested on their knowledge with questions drawn from every intellectual discipline. One contestant has been winning every week for the last three months and is still answering every question correctly. One of the businessmen looks at the other and says, "He is incredible. He knows absolutely everything. How much would you pay him to work in your company?" The other man answers, "Six hundred dollars as a one-time payment for the rest of his life." "Why do you say that?" his friend asks. "Because that is how much a set of encyclopedias costs."

Our minds are not meant to be crammed only with various facts, degrees, and exams. They are for thinking up new ideas and approaches and solving problems. The highly successful people that I know all practice and understand the attitudes and beliefs discussed in this book: self-reliance, courage, creativity, invincible self-confidence, initiative, self-belief, and self-motivation. All the education in the world will not help you achieve your goals if you do not have the initiative, courage and motivation to apply it. Genghis Khan could not read or write, and the Mongols had no administrative skills. However, the Chinese were masters of administration and so he recruited their entire civil service to run his empire for him. He knew that his talents lay in the abilities that allowed him to build an empire and he did not waste his time thinking he had to be able to learn it all himself.

So if you are reading this book and you are not very good at taking exams, or you left school with no qualifications, smile because you are in good company. I could introduce you to countless extremely successful people who are exactly the same. Furthermore, if you came to me for a job interview your exam results would be the last thing I would ask you about. I would want to know about your passions, your goals, how you overcame problems in your life and what you wanted to achieve. Character is more important than straight As. Exam results are easy to acquire; courage and confidence are not.

It is these precious attributes that are essential if we are to learn the next lesson that Genghis Khan teaches us when we look at the injustices he had to endure throughout the early years of his life: that no matter how unfairly you feel you've been treated, take responsibility for your life.

Take Responsibility For Your Life

When I began to study the lives of people I admire, I was struck by the fact that every one of them had gone through incredible hardships to become the person they did, hardships that would have crushed most of us. People who give up on the things that are important to them in life always seem to think that bad things only ever happen to them. They look at successful people as static entities at the height of their fame, surrounded by a frame of their success, but do not ask where they came from and how they got where they are now. I have noticed something about the people I know personally who have achieved great things: it was only after knowing them for years that I found out that some of them had actually overcome serious hardships. One had a debilitating disease that had to be battled daily; another lost her parents when she was very young; and a businessman I respect had been wiped out in business twice before making his fortune. When the subject came up in each case they dismissed it and carried on with the original conversation. Their unspoken attitude was "Life happens, get over it, and move on." This is the opposite of the people I know that have not achieved what they wanted. If you accidentally mention their hardships, you had better have an hour to spare, as once they start on their catalogue of woes it is hard to get away. They know the subject by heart and have excuses for everything, and the constant theme running through it is that it was everybody else's fault; the government, their boss, whoever fits the bill. Anybody and everybody's fault but theirs. The irony is that most of the disasters "other people" caused in their lives were rarely as bad as the hardships experienced by people who got over them and did well. The same event that stopped them in their tracks caused another person to succeed. One person's excuse is another person's reason. I once heard an excuse defined as "A thin shell of truth stuffed with a lie." There is nothing more boring than excuses, so if you want to achieve your goals, stop making them.

The essential characteristics of someone who succeeds in life is that they accept responsibility for themselves, their lives, and their actions. Relying on a third party to bail you out every time you get into trouble is very dangerous. It robs you of your dignity and erodes your character. Yet in many ways in this country we are conditioned to think that if we fall, it is somehow our right to be saved. If we trip then there is somebody that we can sue. The one thing that strikes me about the people I meet when I am on expeditions in the remote regions of the world is their incredible toughness and resourcefulness. Despite the fact that in material terms they have nothing and live in conditions that would be unthinkable for people in the West, they have a charismatic dignity and self-reliance that I rarely see at home. In the tribes that I traveled with in Kashmir, each member is responsible for him or herself and for the other people in the village. If things go wrong there is no one else outside the tribe for them to turn to, no one to help them. As a result they have a strong sense of community, as they know that ultimately their lives are their own responsibilities. This trait is also shared by the people in our culture who achieve greatness and contribute to our society. If you take ownership of your life, your emotions, and your experiences, you move from being a victim into a state of self-empowerment. The minute you start blaming other people then you will effectively rob yourself of the inner resources you need to get yourself out of the situation. This does not mean that we beat ourselves up and take the blame for everything that goes wrong in our lives. Taking responsibility for your life and self-blame are not the same things. Responsibility means that we accept emotionally that the only person who can get us to where we want to go is ourself. Refusing to take responsibility and blaming others hides this truth from us and paralyzes our resolve.

I know all this may sound harsh and that very often in life things happen that are not our fault and can fill us with a deep sense of injustice, but what choice do you have? You can't wallow in the injustice for ever. This is another one of the reasons I find reading the lives of the giants of history so revealing and inspiring, as in many cases the injustices they suffered were the very reasons they became great. It was striving to get away from the harshness of his life and the repeated betrayals that drove Temuchin to become Genghis Khan. It can be the same for you. Studying history teaches us a sobering lesson. Life is not fair. It never has been fair and it never will be fair, but you have a choice. You can decide to work on your self-image (as we discussed in chapter one) so that you can become bigger than the challenges life throws at you, or you can become one of those bitter bores who constantly complain about how unfair life is. This lesson from history toughens us up and can be summed up in the philosophy: "I was born alone and I will die alone. My life is mine and no one else can carry me. Ultimately it is up to me." This belief sounds hard, and the responsibility it carries scares most people, but look around you: do you want to follow the crowd or make your own way?

Success Is the Best Exorcist

What is the opposite of love?

Think about it for a moment.

Did you say hate? Most people do. No, the opposite of love is indifference. People who love each other often, when they hurt each other, switch to hating each other with equal passion, only to fall back in love when they make up. But when a person professes that they are totally indifferent to someone, then all the love and intense emotion that was ever there is gone and the relationship is over. Anger and rage are understood in our culture to be inherently negative emotions, but they are not as bad as apathy and indifference. Anger can be a very healthy reaction when we look at injustices in the world or when we develop our self-image and begin to grow and realize that we have squandered the years and opportunities that were given to us. Anger is one of the greatest motivators we have and we should not try to deny it but channel it. Genghis Khan is an extreme example of the incredibly motivating power of anger. The reason that it produced such destruction was because he did not have the cultural values or knowledge to use it constructively. Here is another powerful example that we can relate to. Florence Nightingale "the lady with the lamp" and the inventor of our modern concept of nursing, worked selflessly during the horrors of the Crimean War. She was up to her elbows in blood and gore, yet never ceased to help the soldiers whose suffering she felt compelled to alleviate. When she was asked why she did it, she gave a one-word answer: "Rage."

I remember reading in a book about ice mountain climbing that a good attitude was not necessarily a positive one, but rather an attitude that got the job done, whether that attitude was fear, anger, or any other emotion that we would normally label as negative. Many self-development books talk about positive mental attitude and the power of positive emotions in achieving great dreams. This is of course true, but is not in my opinion a real reflection of life for most people. The reason why many people become cynical about the whole subject of motivation, be it motivational books or speakers, is because very rarely is the subject explained fully. Deep down everyone in life wants to be happy and do well in a way that is relevant and significant to them. Unfortunately, the subject of motivation is most often reduced to Rah Rah pep talks and empty clichés like "If you believe you are a winner, then you are a winner." That statement, although often true at heart, is very irritating and overly simplistic. Furthermore, the idea that to succeed you have to have a permanent smile on your face is very hard for most people to relate to.

Like Florence Nightingale, many of the hugely successful business people I know were driven by inner rage, fear, or a need to prove themselves born out of insecurity. Most of them are very nice people, but their driving motivation in life was provided by a very negative emotion. Interestingly, the achievement of their goal often acted as a catharsis that drove out their demon and exorcized the fear, rage, or insecurities that drove them, replacing it with a calm wisdom and self-knowledge. It is my experience and the evidence of history that this drive harnessed properly can be one of the most powerful motivators in human nature. So if you feel scared, resentful, or angry you have two choices: you can either do nothing and let your emotion fester until it eats you alive; or you can use it to drive you and by creating a better life for yourself exorcise it from your system. But whatever you do, realize that you do not necessarily have to be happy all the time to achieve your goals. Just be yourself and be willing to grow, that's all you need.

Business Lessons from the Great Khan

Genghis Khan not only teaches us how anyone can rise to greatness despite horrendous odds and a disadvantaged background, but a great deal more. His ideas that turned a chaotic, mutually hostile band of horsemen into the most efficient army the world had ever seen can show us how to structure organizations today.

MERITOCRACIES CREATE STRONG ORGANIZATIONS

In the Second World War, the Germans fighting on the Eastern Front were amazed that despite the horrendous casualties the Russians were suffering, they still managed to produce officers of outstanding quality who commanded the respect of their common soldiers. The reason was simple: the communist state, despite its many flaws, was a meritocracy, and the men who became officers had started out as common soldiers. They had worked their way up the ranks and as a result had earned their position through their merits. This was in stark contrast to the many second-rate upper-class officers that class-ridden Britain produced in the First World War.

Barrier to entry based on a person's background, race, or any reason other than individual merit is not only morally wrong but is extremely inefficient, bad for morale, and, most dangerously, can result in mediocre people being promoted to positions of leadership. I have seen this repeatedly in companies, and the results are usually disastrous. When a company has the owner's best friend's son at the head of it, I always want to know if he has had to work his way up from the bottom or been handed the key position on a plate. If he has started at the top then I know that he will probably be arrogant, way out of his depth, and his staff will not respect him. Furthermore, when that company confronts a vigorous, lean competitor that promotes on merit, the resulting clash is not simply one of competition for market share, but that of their cultures. This is exactly what happened when the Mongol hordes confronted the arrogance of the armies of China and Europe. So many business organizations crumble because of their arrogance and the weakness of their culture. Strong societies and companies are made up of strong individuals. A person who expects advancement in life by relying on a family name, school tie, or postcode displays a distinct lack of character and an inability to stand on his or her own merits. When the tests in life come, our character is revealed and nothing else will see us through. Our character is our true identity and it is there that we should place our faith.

One of Genghis Khan's most outstanding gifts was his uncanny ability to pick the right person for the job regardless of their background. Unlike Alexander the Great, he had absolutely no interest in personal heroics and never led charges himself. He very astutely saw his success as being dependent on the quality of his officers, and as a result rewarded excellence and promoted talent wherever he found it. His promotion of the archer Jebe who nearly killed him in battle shows a wisdom and lack of vindictiveness that contradicts his vengeful nature. He was so committed to this policy that he was said never to have made a mistake in appointing the right man to the job. As a result it was his brilliant generals who were responsible for his most spectacular victories and campaigns. But it was not just Genghis Khan's meritocratic approach that created outstanding generals in his army, he also let others take the glory.

LET OTHERS TAKE THE GLORY

I dealt with a guy in business once and I had to stifle a smile every time I walked into his office. He had designed it as a shrine . . . to himself. As you walked in, all the walls were covered in pictures of him receiving awards, meeting celebrities, playing golf, etc. These were interspersed with his qualifications, no matter how small. His huge throne sat behind a huge desk that of course was elevated to look down on the rickety little chair that was provided for visitors. The irony was that he was a really nice guy who meant well, but he had inadvertently created a little theater with him as the star. He had some really talented young people who worked there but they all gradually left. They were not allowed to grow or shine because he was the star of the show. He did not realize he was exerting that pressure and despite his good intentions he was left with a company full of people with no initiative. There was just no room for anyone else's talent to shine.

One of the most valuable lessons I learned from the mentors mentioned in chapter one is that the role of a leader in business (and in many other fields) is to create an environment that nurtures excellence in their staff or team mates. One of the most memorable things one of them said to me was "Michael, I don't believe that you work for me. I believe that I work for you and it is my job to ensure that you have everything you need to nurture your talents and do your best." He knew that if he helped me to do my best, then he would achieve his aims. This was exactly the opposite approach to those of the small-minded middle managers who had been my bosses in my first jobs. Their limited thinking meant that they were too preoccupied building their tiny empires within the company. It was not in their interests to let their staff shine too much. The difference in thinking between the desk-bound, average-wage middle managers and the self-made millionaires was striking.

One of the qualities necessary in managers who encourage excellence in their team is a deep sense of self-confidence and a lack of ego. This is one of the more admirable qualities demonstrated by Genghis Khan, and is remarkable when we consider the sheer size of his achievements. World conquerors are usually characterized by their egomania. It was this willingness to take a back seat that was responsible for his empire's exponential expansion. By allowing spectacular generals to come to the fore and encouraging and rewarding initiative in his own men, he created a culture that drew out the best in his subordinates. Even though the succession to the throne of Great Khan was limited to his descendants, he picked the son who he believed would be the best, despite the fact that he was not the oldest. As discussed, Genghis Khan's army structure was meritocratic, and the common soldiers could therefore see the bravery of their peers being rewarded around them. This encouraged every soldier to do his best and created a robust and dynamic culture.

So one of the key components of leadership that we can learn from Genghis Khan is to let others have the limelight and allow their talents to breathe. But he did not encourage ambition to grow unfettered. He had one rule that you transgressed at your peril.

99.9 PERCENT LOYALTY IS 100 PERCENT DISLOYALTY

If history teaches us anything, it is that no matter how big your army is, if it is not loyal it will be scattered and defeated by a smaller force if the latter is more loyal to their leader. Alexander the Great demonstrated this when his fanatically loyal Macedonians repeatedly scattered the Persian conscripts, and Genghis Khan's Mongol hordes also defeated vastly superior forces because of their cohesiveness and devoted loyalty to each other and their leader. The same applies today, whether it is a football team or a large blue-chip company.

If there is an atmosphere of distrust the effect on the company is disastrous, even in smaller companies. People spend most of their time trying to work out if their position is secure rather than feeling free to contribute to the financial well-being of the company. Loyalty is not an easy thing to create, but you can achieve more with five motivated, loyal staff than you can with fifty demotivated, disloyal ones. Motivation and loyalty go hand in hand. I have experienced this repeatedly in my life. As a result I am never intimidated by large competitors. Experience has taught me that the staff of large companies are rarely encouraged to be loyal and their leaders rarely earn loyalty. Here's an example. I once approached a huge British company and asked their communications department if I could borrow a piece of equipment that they manufactured for an expedition I was going on. The promotional benefits they would have received would have been enormous and too long to list here. Their PR manager was delighted and said he wanted to get involved. However, two months later he told me sheepishly that he could not support the project as the department that supplied the equipment was fighting with him and had refused to lend it in order to spite him. Can you believe that? Very rarely do I encounter large organizations that are not afflicted by chronic disloyalty and infighting. It makes competing with them a lot easier, as when they experience external pressure the infighting gets worse and they often tear themselves apart.

However, if I am confronted by a company, even if it is considerably smaller than mine, with a committed leader who cares for the people who work for him and earns their loyalty, I always pause and think twice. If they are bonded together by more than the fact that it is their job, then competing with them can be much harder than the size of their company would suggest. I have encountered companies where the staff feel that by not doing their best they are actually letting their friends down. Their job and their company are aligned with the higher needs and values that were discussed in chapter one.

Many companies make the mistake of thinking that simply paying large salaries will ensure loyalty and motivation, but again if you study history you will see that the least reliable troops are mercenaries. Money does not buy loyalty. Disloyal troops will run at the first chance they get, but loyal ones will fight till the end.

The reason that so many staff are not particularly loyal to

the company they work for is because business leaders rarely try to earn the loyalty of the people who make their company work. The emotions that nurture loyalty are not encouraged or sought out. Many leaders expect or demand loyalty without ever earning it and rarely engage their staff as people rather than workers. If you don't give a damn for your staff, why should they give a damn for you?

SUPERIOR TECHNOLOGY DEFEATS PERSONAL HEROICS

If your competitor has superior technology, or if a new technology has been launched, heroics won't save you. When the car was invented it would have been heroic but stupid for a saddle-maker to think he could fight it. It would have been far wiser for him to decide to cater to a smaller market, or start using his leather expertise to diversify and make upholstery for cars. Only a fool tries to stop the tide from coming in. Often I see companies in the face of new technology putting on a brave face and proclaiming that they will fight it. This is ludicrous and pointless and is a futile way to spend your talents. It is far better to study the way the tide is going and endeavor to align your goals with it. The history of the wars of the Mongols is littered with brave last stands and heroic charges by their enemies, but the fact remains that in the face of vastly superior strategies and technology, heroics only leads you to a quicker death.

Genghis Khan's flight from lifelong threats and his revenge-taking give us an excellent insight into the power of fear in human motivation. His formation of the Mongol nation and their lethal military machine can teach us about how to structure companies and organizations in a modern setting.

But Genghis Khan and the Mongol hordes also taught us something else: how to completely out-think our competitors. However, rather than learning this lesson from Genghis Khan, it is better that we learn it from the master, the man who wrote the book on outwitting your competitors by doing the unthinkable. It is time to meet Hannibal.

3

Hannibal

Thunderbolt

The clanking sound of armor echoed through the temple as the soldiers marched through the flickering torchlight. As they drew close to the altar, a distinguished warrior emerged from their ranks, leading a small boy by the hand. Standing beneath the statue of the god Melqart, he drew his dagger and performed the sacrifice that had been prepared for him. As the incense filled the air, he gently took the boy's hand and placed it in the blood that seeped across the altar. Kneeling, he looked earnestly into the child's eyes. "Tomorrow we leave for Spain to carve a new homeland for our people. Swear with me, Hannibal, before the god Melqart, that as long as you live you will be the enemy of Rome." The boy remembered the agony and humiliation his father had suffered at the hands of the Romans' treachery and in that moment promised that he would never yield to them. "I swear, Father, I swear it."

Hannibal Barca was born in 247 B.C. in the merchant city-state of Carthage, in the modern-day Gulf of Tunis. The Barca family were powerful members of the Carthaginian aristocracy and had produced many of Carthage's greatest military commanders. Even their family name, Barca meant "Thunderbolt," and from a young age Hannibal was bred for war. He would live up to his name and continue the family tradition by becoming one of the greatest generals that ever lived. The day he was born, his father assumed supreme command of the Carthaginian forces, a position that Hannibal would inherit as Carthage fought to preserve its freedom in the rising shadow of the most ruthless power the Mediterranean had ever seen . . . Rome. It was to oppose this power that Hannibal would devote his whole life and so keep the promise that he made to his father as a young boy in the temple.

The Punic Wars

The Carthaginians were the entrepreneurs of the ancient world, and their business interests included not only the Mediterranean but also a vast area from Britain and the Baltic to the north and as far as central Africa to the south. Carthage was a city-state and operated in the same way as the independent Greek city-states. As a result it did not have the population nor desire to be a large military power and create an empire. The people of Carthage simply wanted a peaceful life so that they could get on with their trading. The Romans, however, were different. Despite repeatedly signing treaties that outlined their respective territories, the Romans continued to break their word and expand aggressively.

When they threatened the Carthaginian naval bases in Sicily, Carthage had no choice but to go reluctantly to war to ensure their survival. Hannibal's father, Hamilcar, led the Carthaginians in this war that would be known as the First Punic War (247–241 B.C.). It ended when Carthage was defeated at a disastrous naval battle. Despairing, they sued for peace and were forced to surrender their strategic bases in Malta and Sicily and pay crippling war reparations. But Hannibal's father believed that Carthage had surrendered too easily and he knew that the Romans could not be trusted.

His judgement was to be proved correct. Despite the peace treaty that had been inflicted upon Carthage, the Romans continued to expand. Hamilcar knew that the writing was on the wall and that before long the ambitions of Rome would envelop Carthage itself. Faced with this fate, he took the previously unthinkable step for a sea-faring culture and invaded Spain in an attempt to build an empire to rival that of Rome. He took his nine-year-old son Hannibal, to Spain with him. It would become Hannibal's home, and seventeen years later, at the age of twenty-six, he assumed command of the Carthaginian army there.

However, it did not take long for the Romans to notice the growing colonial power of Carthage and begin to meddle in their affairs. But this time they had Hannibal to deal with. He deliberately thwarted their attempts to expand into Spain and played them at their own game. Enraged, the Romans demanded that the Carthaginians hand Hannibal over to them. When they were refused, they declared war. But the Romans were blinded by their arrogance. Because of their overwhelming supremacy at sea, they thought that Hannibal was trapped in Spain and that victory was inevitable. To claim it they immediately despatched an army to invade Spain and capture him.

Elephants over the Alps

That was exactly what Hannibal wanted them to do. He had already prepared to leave Spain. Unable to transport his army by sea, he would lead his 51,000 infantry, 9,000 cavalry and 37 elephants through northern Spain, across the Pyrenees, through France and then, inconceivably, over the high Alpine passes in winter to invade Italy. It was the most daring military campaign in history. Hannibal was going to avenge his father and attack Rome itself. This was the first time that the Romans would fall into one of Hannibal's ingenious traps, but it would not be the last.

The march was a living hell. The Carthaginians had to defend themselves against the ferocious Gallic tribes of northern Spain and France. In the mountains the tribes attacked them relentlessly, launching boulders to crush the men from above. But their worst enemy was the winter conditions in the high mountain passes. Men and animals plummeted to their deaths over ravines, and only through Hannibal's inspired leadership did they succeed. The statistics reveal the true horror of the journey. Only half of the 60,000 men who left Spain with Hannibal made it to Italy.

When news arrived in Rome that Hannibal had appeared out of nowhere there was panic in the streets. Appropriately, the people talked of his descent "like a thunderbolt" from the mountains. What they did not know was that his bedraggled army was half starved and frostbitten and in no fit state to fight anyone.

First blood was drawn in Italy at the battle of the Trebia in 218 B.C. Two Roman legions were sent to confront Hannibal, under the dual leadership of the consuls Scipio and Sempronius. Sempronius was highly ambitious and wanted to take the credit for defeating Hannibal alone. In doing so he rushed straight into one of Hannibal's traps and was responsible for the total destruction of the two legions he had led. In any other situation the rag-tag army that had invaded Italy would have been scattered by the disciplined legions, but for one essential detail: Hannibal was their leader.

Hannibal's Leadership Style

Historical records suggest a large number of similarities between Hannibal's style of leadership and that of Alexander the Great. Like Alexander, Hannibal was of aristocratic birth and was raised to be a soldier. He was extremely charming and courteous and carried himself with the calm self-confidence of somebody who was in complete control of their actions. He is said to have been willing to put himself through great physical hardship and to disdain comfort: he was often catching moments of sleep wrapped in a military cloak at sentry posts, and eating only when he had to. He also dressed like his soldiers and was always the first into battle and the last to leave it. Also, like Alexander, he was very courteous to women who were captured after battle, and was said to have possessed the same God-given talent for leadership and the ability to inspire devotion and loyalty in his troops. When we look at these striking similarities, it is no surprise to learn that Hannibal believed Alexander to be the greatest general who had ever lived.

But in some ways, the task of leading his men was harder for Hannibal than it had been for Alexander. Hannibal's army was a jumbled mix of North African and Spanish soldiers and French and Italian mercenary tribesmen, the latter were wild, undisciplined, and only interested in plundering the settlements of the Romans who had suppressed them. A fascinating account of one of his pre-battle speeches demonstrates brilliantly how he dealt with this. Before the battle of Trebia, Hannibal instructed the entire army to assemble in a circle. The motley gathering spoke a multitude of dialects and languages and had different motivations for being there. So rather than attempting to make a rousing speech, he had a number of prisoners taken from the tribes of Gaul who had attacked them during their march. They were given the choice of either remaining slaves or fighting each other in a gladiatorial contest. The victor would be given his freedom, money, armor, and a horse. The loser would at least be spared his present suffering. All agreed to the gladiatorial contest. Once it was over, the dead were dragged away and the victors were presented with their reward, and those who had not been given the chance to fight, were led away in chains. Hannibal had just used a powerful and emotive demonstration to explain their situation: that if they fought and won, the riches of Rome were theirs; but if they lost, then either the pain of death or the misery of slaves awaited them. A brutal lesson for brutal times, but everyone assembled got the message.

But Hannibal's brilliant leadership style is not the reason that he is renowned in history, nor is it the reason that I was compelled to include him in this book. No, Hannibal's genius lay in his ability to consistently out-think his opponents, and repeatedly take them by surprise.

Hannibal's Tactics

Hannibal's brilliance is demonstrated in his consistent creativity in devising ingenious strategies and methods for achieving his aims, regardless of his environment or circumstances. He exploited every component of a situation, from the personality of his opponent to the geographic terrain, and turned them to his advantage. The Romans constantly complained that in warfare he did not play by the rules, but what they did not understand was that he was simply centuries ahead of his time and thought like a modern general. Here are some of the best examples of his tactics.

Hannibal's army was a ragtag group of Gallic tribesmen, mercenaries, and professional soldiers from Spain and North Africa. The most volatile and unpredictable of these were the Gauls. Hannibal's brother-in-law had been killed by one of them over an unspecified grievance, and Hannibal knew that he would be the target of a number of assassination attempts by the tribes he had subdued on his way to Italy. The whole Italian campaign relied on his survival, but rather than employing a huge number of bodyguards, Hannibal had a series of wigs made in various styles and colors, and outfits to match them. He changed his appearance on a day-to-day basis, a tactic that was so effective that no one in his army, never mind his enemies, could agree on what he looked like, and even his close friends had trouble recognizing him.

Hannibal is most famous for his daring crossing of the Alps on elephants, but what is not widely known is that he repeated a similar maneuver while in Italy. After the battle of Trebia, the Roman armies were prepared and waiting for him along the most obvious routes to Rome. Hannibal would never fight on the ground or terms that his opponents had chosen, and so in another move of breathtaking daring he led his army through the marshes of a place called the Lower Arno. The ordeal meant that his men could not sleep for days as they were marching through water sometimes up to their waists. The only thing that drove them forward was the sight of Hannibal on his elephant leading them on. The conditions were so inhospitable that Hannibal caught an infection that resulted in him losing the sight in one eye, but the plan paid off and Hannibal's armies were free to plunder the rich lands of Tuscany uncontested.

But there was a deeper strategy behind that of simply allowing his men to enjoy the fruits of their enemy's land. Hannibal knew that Flaminius, the Roman consul who had been waiting to bar his way, was of similar temperament to Sempronius, whom he had previously defeated at Trebia: an arrogant egoist who would not be able to bear the public humiliation of himself or Rome. Flaminius's officers advised him to wait for the other armies to arrive, but the consul wanted to be seen as the sole champion and savior of Rome. Exactly as Hannibal had planned, Flaminius took the bait and raced off to attack the Carthaginians, and in so doing led his legions into a trap that resulted in Hannibal's second annihilation of the Romans.

Hannibal set his trap at Lake Trasimene, a U-shaped valley with the lake running along one side. In his hands it was terrain designed for slaughter. He arranged his main force at the end of the valley, to entice the Romans, but hid the Gauls and his heavy cavalry in the mists of the slope opposite the lake. As the Romans entered the valley and saw their enemy at the head of it, they were eager to engage them, but before they knew it, the trumpets roared and the cavalry emerged from the mists and trapped them in the valley. Hannibal attacked from the front, while the mass of screaming Gauls attacked from the side, forcing the Romans into the lake. Three hours later, 15,000 Romans, including Flaminius, were dead. It was the greatest military setback the Romans had ever suffered.

At this point the Romans realized that they would have to make drastic changes to deal with Hannibal. Part of the reason why they had been so easily trapped by him in the last two battles was their political structure. The consular system of the republic meant that two consuls commanded two legions each and served alongside one another for a year before being replaced. Even more democratically, when the consuls were together they took turns at commanding the four legions, swapping command each day. This was a situation that Hannibal had exploited to the full. In both battles, the consuls had been lured to their destruction because they had wanted to take all the credit for the victory. Such a system was too dangerous when facing a general like Hannibal, and so the Romans took the previously unthinkable step of appointing a dictator by election. The man chosen was the highly respected Quintus Fabius Maximus, or "The Delayer," as he was later to be nicknamed. Fabius knew that the way to deal with a military genius like Hannibal was quite simply not to fight him. By avoiding battle and harassing Hannibal as he tried to find food for his army, Fabius was ironically suggesting that the Romans conduct a guerrilla campaign against an enemy in their own country. He was wise enough to realize that Hannibal's weakness lay in the fact that he had to live off the land, and that by harassing it rather than confronting it, he would wear down the Carthaginian army and cause them to lose morale. He was right, and Hannibal knew it.

As would be expected, Hannibal, realizing the temperament of his new enemy, found a way of using it against him. He commanded his troops to lay waste to all the lands they encountered, but whenever they came across lands belonging to Fabius or his family they conspicuously left them untouched. This had two effects on the proud Romans: first, they grew more and more impatient with Fabius's delaying tactics as they watched Hannibal destroy their lands unchallenged; and second, they began to believe that Fabius was being bribed by Hannibal. The last straw for the Romans came when it seemed as if Fabius and his legions actually had Hannibal trapped at Campania. Hannibal had camped on a large plain in an attempt to draw Fabius into a battle, but Fabius wisely decided to place his troops in the hills surrounding the plain and block all the escape routes. Hannibal was trapped, and even the cautious Fabius was optimistic. However, he did not know that Hannibal had already planned his escape. He ordered his troops to tie torches to the horns of thousands of their cattle. When night came, they lit them and began to drive them over the ridge and down on to the Romans below. The legionnaires, believing they were being outflanked, rushed out to attack the enemy, but were astounded to find a herd of cattle instead. Hearing the commotion, Fabius assumed they were being attacked as well, but as Hannibal had foreseen, his cautious nature would not allow him to take any action until daylight, and so while the Romans waited with bated breath behind their stockades, Hannibal led his army effortlessly through the pass at the other side of the plain.

To the Roman army and the citizens of Rome, Hannibal's escape was just another example of the failure of Fabius's policy. In desperation, the dual consular system was reestablished and the two positions were occupied by Consuls Paulus and Varro. It was exactly the situation Hannibal wanted. Little did they know it, but the Romans' decision to abandon the policy of avoiding Hannibal in battle would bring about the worst calamity ever to befall the republic.

The Battle of Cannea—216 B.C.

Hannibal watched as the Roman legions marched into formation before him. He had been thwarted by the cautious delaying tactics of Fabius, but now, at long last, the Romans had brought their entire army to face him: 80,000 men against his 40,000. The battle that was about to unfold would be Hannibal's masterpiece.

Hannibal had already recruited nature to his cause. By choosing his position wisely, he had forced the Romans to move away from their water supplies. The merciless summer heat was baking them in their armor, and already the sun was in their eyes. A sirocco wind was blowing up the Adriatic coast and lazily puffing the dust of the plain into the legionnaires' faces, making them cough. The legions began to advance towards Hannibal using exactly the same formation as they always did, relying on the strength of their heavy infantry to try and punch their way through his lines. In their last encounters he had noticed how the disciplined, stout legionnaires had repeatedly bested the Gallic tribesmen. The Gauls were recklessly brave but savagely undisciplined and no match for the tightly knit Roman formations. To combat this, Hannibal had placed the naked, painted Gauls in the very center of his lines: his weakest troops against their strongest. Behind them, on both the left and right flanks, facing inwards, he placed his elite African heavy infantry keeping them in reserve. As line upon line of the legions approached, it became apparent that the Gauls of the Carthaginian center were formed in a convex semicircle that protruded curiously out toward the Romans. A formation that was inherently weak.

As the first wave clashed, the Gauls, screaming their war cries, fell upon the Romans with savage fury, but very soon the relentless force of the massed legions began to force them back. First they buckled, then their line began to bend inwards, forming a U-shape. The Roman soldiers, encouraged by their "victory," poured through the gaps in the Carthaginian center like water through a burst dam. So eager were they to attack the retreating Gauls that they began to crush one another, moving slowly, oblivious to the African heavy infantry that stood silently, like dark shadows, on their flanks. The moment had arrived. Over the screaming, the trumpet sounded the signal, and the heavy African infantry began to advance from either side, crushing the Romans in a vice. The Romans were trapped, with the Gauls to their front, the cavalry to their rear and the battle-fresh Africans attacking from both sides.

Seventy thousand Romans were killed that day, including

more than half of their nobility, among them eighty senators. The historian Livy wrote that "No other nation could have suffered such a tremendous disaster and not been destroyed." Hannibal's father and the humiliation of Carthage had been avenged. He had achieved his audacious plan of attacking the heart of the Roman Empire and bringing it to its knees. Now Rome would capitulate and beg for peace.

The Face of Fortitude

But they didn't. Despite the fact that every family in Rome had lost fathers, brothers, and sons to the revenge of Hannibal, despite the fact that they were helpless in the face of his military genius and that his makeshift army could roam wherever and whenever they wished, the Romans quite simply refused to give in. They gritted their teeth and introduced draconian measures to cope with the crisis: public mourning was forbidden, and talking in public places was banned to prevent gossip and rumors; all messengers to the city were forbidden to discuss their information with the public; more legions were raised, and a crippling tax was imposed to pay for the war effort. This response showed the difference in character between the Romans and the Carthaginians, or indeed any other ancient culture. The Carthaginians' spirit had been broken, forcing them to sue for peace, after only one small defeat in the First Punic War (a capitulation for which Hannibal's father never forgave his countrymen), and in the case of Alexander the Great, the Persian Empire had collapsed after only three major battles, but the Romans were made of sterner stuff. And it was this stern face that they turned to him now that would ultimately be Hannibal's undoing and earn the Romans the right to found their enduring empire.

Hannibal was at an utter loss about what to do next. He had excelled and achieved all his goals, but the Romans had defied convention and logic and continued to resist him. More worrying for him was the tragic irony that his spectacular victories had exposed his fatal weakness: quite simply that he did not know what to do with his victories. Hannibal had no political will or plan for the future. He simply wanted to return the status quo to the days before the First Punic War when Carthage had been the commercial master of the Mediterranean. He wanted nothing more than to turn the clock back. It is a telling indictment of his lack of political vision that despite the crushing defeats he inflicted on the Roman Republic, not one of the member regions in their federation deserted Rome to join him. They knew that the might of Rome was on the ascent and that Hannibal was a general of the old school who was not in touch with the new world order. But even more alarming for Hannibal was the fact that after years of grueling defeats, the Romans had begun to study his tactics and learn from them. The pain he inflicted on them forced them to change the way they thought about war completely and about how to fight battles. This new approach was to have two disastrous effects on Hannibal, both personally and militarily.

"I See There the Fate of Carthage"

The first disaster occurred in the year 207 B.C. when it actually looked as if Hannibal was finally going to force the Romans to surrender. Realizing that if he did not defeat

Rome once and for all he would eventually be driven from Italy, he decided to intensify the pressure and had sent for his brother, Hasdrubal, to join him. Hasdrubal was an outstanding general in his own right, and upon receiving his brother's request he left Spain with his army and entered Italy via the same route as Hannibal, over the Alps. When news reached Rome that Hannibal was to their south and a new army under his brother was advancing from the north, there was panic in the streets. "The Lions' Brood," as the Romans called the brothers, once united would almost certainly devour Rome, and the Senate knew that the brothers had to be prevented from joining their forces at all costs. Despite the terror that Hannibal and Hasdrubal inspired in them, the Romans steeled themselves and faced the threat with such courage and dignity that later generations looked to this period as a great inspiration.

The Romans knew that they were probably doomed, but as often happens in life, fortune smiled on them when least expected and a letter from Hasdrubal arranging where the armies should meet was intercepted. Upon reading it, the consul Claudius Nero acted with decisive brilliance. Taking a small force, he raced to join the second consular army that was waiting to face Hasdrubal, leaving the remainder of his army to block Hannibal. He sent riders ahead to inform all the towns and villages that the fate of the Republic was at stake and to have food and water waiting for the soldiers as they marched past. The roads were soon lined with citizens showering food and supplies on the marching columns, and this romantic image became an enduring myth of one of Rome's finest hours. Claudius Nero had learned his lessons well from Hannibal, and when he reached the other consular army's camp he instructed his soldiers not to pitch their tents but to share the tents of the other soldiers that were already pitched there. By doing this he tricked Hasdrubal into thinking that he still faced one army instead of two. Little did Hasdrubal know that the army he faced had doubled in size overnight. The next day, Claudius Nero inflicted a crushing defeat upon Hasdrubal, and in doing so, saved Rome from possible extinction.

Far to the south, Hannibal was oblivious of the disaster that had befallen his brother. The first he knew of it was when some Roman cavalry rode to his camp and threw a sack at his sentries. When it was brought to Hannibal in his tent he looked in it and said simply "I see there the fate of Carthage." In it was the head of his younger brother. Hannibal was to remain in Italy for a further four years and was never defeated, but with the death of his brother and his army dwindling he knew that his dream of defeating Rome by striking at her heart was at an end.

Imitation—The Highest Form of Flattery

The second consequence of Rome's willingness to learn from Hannibal came in the form of his great adversary-to-be, Publius Cornelius Scipio. Scipio was an exceptionally talented soldier who had suffered personally at the hands of Hannibal. He had been one of the bloodied legionnaires who had managed to escape the destruction at Cannea. Yet rather than succumbing to despair, he had shown his mettle and rallied his countrymen when they felt that all resistance to Hannibal was hopeless. Scipio used Hannibal's years in Italy to study and learn from him and experimented with

"Hannibalistic" tactics to great success. When he was ready he moved to implement the greatest lesson he had learned from his antagonist and mentor. He would attack him in a way that would ensure that he would leave Italy. If he could not defeat Hannibal in Italy he would use his own master tactic against him and play Hannibal at his own game: Scipio would invade Carthage.

The plan worked. In the spring of 204 B.C., Scipio and his legions disembarked at Cape Farina, near Carthage. In the autumn of the following year Hannibal left Italy to return to Carthage and save it. The greatest testament to the power of Hannibal is that even after sixteen years he left Italy of his own accord, not because he was driven out by the Romans. In 202 B.C. Scipio and Hannibal met again on the battlefield of Zama, near Carthage but this time it was Hannibal who was at a disadvantage. He was desperately short of both cavalry and experienced troops, and Scipio was now his match in battlefield tactics and generalship. The disadvantages were such that even Hannibal could not compensate for them and he was defeated on a battlefield for the first and last time. The Second Punic War was over. Rome had won, not in Italy but in Africa.

After the War

The Roman victory at Zama brought an end to seventeen long years of war. Many in Rome wanted Hannibal dragged back to the city in chains, but Scipio, who had developed an intense admiration for him, prevented this. Despite the jealousy of his enemies, Scipio was the man of the hour (he was even awarded the name Scipio "Africanus" by the Romans, after the continent he had defeated). He knew that without strong leadership Carthage would fall apart, and he knew the man he wanted for the job. With Scipio's blessing, Hannibal was appointed the chief magistrate of Carthage and set about rebuilding the city he had left as a child and spent his whole life fighting for. Hannibal was an incorruptible statesman. He proved himself to be as powerful a leader of a city as he was a general, and rebuilt Carthage into a mercantile power once more. Ironically it was his success that led to his self-imposed exile. Corrupt politicians that he had exposed in Carthage joined forces with those in Rome who hated him. Together they contrived charges that he had been assisting an enemy of Rome, and in 195 B.C. a commission was sent to Carthage to bring him back to Rome to face charges.

But Hannibal, as usual, was already one step ahead of them and escaped. For the remaining thirteen years of his life he lived in the courts of various kingdoms in the Middle East and the Mediterranean. The Romans had made it known throughout the world that he was their enemy and that no man, king, or country was allowed to shelter him. He spent the rest of his life fleeing before the shadow of Rome as it moved over the world.

Eventually he came to the remote kingdom of Bithynia, ruled by King Prusias. Even here in his last years Hannibal showed his genius for the element of surprise. King Prusias was at war with Pergamum, a city-state of Asia Minor that was a client state of Rome. Prusias was losing badly, and he turned to Hannibal for advice. Hannibal managed to turn the course of the war and win a sea battle using a strategy so ingenious that it marks an appropriate end to his brilliant life.

Naval battles of the time were fought in open warships.

Due to the climate and the nature of sea battles, the oarsmen wore very little clothing and even the marines were lightly clad. Hannibal devised the perfect weapon to exploit this. As the enemy ships approached, the Bithynians fired clay jars at them. At first the sailors of Pergamum were bemused by this until they burst open and spilled their contents across the decks. To their horror they saw that they contained poisonous snakes. Instantly there was widespread panic as the sailors jumped overboard, desperately trying to avoid the serpents. Totally demoralized by Hannibal's "snake bombs," they retreated in disarray. With Hannibal's guidance the Bithynians had won without even drawing their swords.

It did not take long for Rome to hear about this unusual victory. Suspicious, the Romans summoned the envoys of King Prusias to Rome to give an account of it, and whilst there one of the envoys let it slip that Hannibal was in their kingdom. . . .

The Final Defiance—183 B.C.

Hannibal had defeated countless Roman legions, yet now that he was alone, those very soldiers surrounded his villa. He knew the fate that awaited him if he fell into the Romans' hands. He looked up to see an anxious servant hovering at the door, "Sir, the soldiers will be here any minute."

Hannibal drew his dagger. "It is now time to end the anxiety of the Romans." And as the life ebbed from him, he smiled in the knowledge that he had never broken his childhood promise, and that Hannibal, the scourge of Rome, would die as he had lived: a free man.

SECTION TWO: LESSONS
WHAT WE CAN LEARN FROM HANNIBAL

The Power of One

Often when we see injustices, tragedies, opportunities, and gifts that life contains, our hearts are moved to pity and the desire to make a difference. We want to help those who are in need, or pursue a dream, and in achieving it thereby make a contribution to the world. Our minds wander, gaining momentum as we picture all the things we could do and say, and the difference we could make. But as soon as we begin to get excited and our hearts steel with resolve, we stop and a voice inside us says, "But what can I do alone when there is only me? What difference can one person make?" And then the dream is gone and our minds accept compromise and return to the mundane matters of the day. I believe that in that moment a part of us, the part that is destined for greatness, dies. The small seed of faith that lies in all of us becomes buried deeper every time we decide that pursuing a precious goal is pointless or futile. Thankfully the converse is also true: if you dare to believe, even for an instant, that what you have dreamed of is possible, that part of you grows a little stronger, and if you nurture that part of you enough, it can change the world. It is when we follow these inner impulses that we feel most alive, most aligned with who we really are. This may sound fanciful, but think about it. Right now, think of all the great historical movements in the world. You will find that the vast majority started in the mind of just one person, who believed enough to inspire a small group of people to believe, who then in turn motivated the rest of us.

Who forced the British to leave India? Gandhi. Who led the Russian Revolution? Lenin and the Bolsheviks. Who unified the Mongol hordes? (You know the answer to that one.) Unfortunately, this sort of passion can have disastrous effects as well, but the lessons of history reveal one simple fact: rather than being powerless, individuals who care enough are the people who have always changed the world, for good or bad.

Hannibal is a perfect example of the power of one person. More so perhaps than all the other characters in this book, as his army was a rag-tag assortment of tribesmen and mercenaries. He did not have the elite Macedonian phalanx or the Mongol horsemen at his disposal. However, his brilliance compensated for that, and he single-handedly brought Rome to her knees.

In this book I have talked a lot about great achievements and enduring passions, of desert battles and the hearts of champions. I understand that you may be saying, "But Michael, I work in a shoe-shop and I don't really want to take over the world." Our lives are much simpler affairs, but our hearts still yearn to feel fully alive and to experience our lives to the full, to feel like the masters of our own destinies, to be the heroes in our own adventures.

So whereas in history there has been one person who changed the world, right now there is only one person who can change your world, your life, and that is you. No matter how small you think your life is, the fact remains the same. It is up to you to change it. No, we may not feel that we can change the world, but we can make a huge difference to our own lives and be an inspiration to those around us. Once you grasp this, the journey becomes so exciting, and I promise you this: in those moments when you have the courage to act on your deepest beliefs and passions, you will know what it means to be alive and why you were put on this earth. Life will have a purpose that it never had before, and when you look back you will be astounded at how far you have come.

I urge you to turn away from indifference and apathy and embrace a life of powerful, compassionate action. No matter where you are in life and no matter what you do, by simply undertaking one small thing each day, week, or even month, you can make such a difference for others and build a deep inner self-respect for yourself. It is better to light one candle than to curse the darkness. If you have the courage to do this, the future will be full of people who will bless your name. As Emerson said "To know even one life has breathed easier because you have lived. This is the meaning of success."

Use your work to make a difference in your life and the lives of those around you. Even if you feel that what you do is beneath you or that you are only doing it to pay the rent, who you are today is the person who will get you to tomorrow, and what you do today is what will build your future. All you have to do is believe that you can change your own world and decide that you will do a little better each day. Once you have helped yourself, then you will be able to turn your attentions to those around you, who will benefit from your wisdom and experience. I use business as my vehicle; where do your talents lie? Remember, the world we live in and take for granted today was built by people who did care, who could be bothered.

Here's a story that always makes me smile and reminds me of how small actions can make a big difference in other people's lives, and how we should never be put off by the feeling that we can't help everyone.

An old man is walking along a beach after a storm when he sees a little boy in the distance. As he approaches him he sees that the storm has washed hundreds of starfish on to the sand. The little boy is running up and down, picking up starfish one at a time, and throwing them back into the sea. The old man cynically smiles to himself at the futility of the child's actions, and as he approaches says "Heh, why don't you go and enjoy yourself? You can't save them all, so what difference will it make throwing one or two back?" The little boy picks up another starfish, and as he sends it flying back to its home, he looks at the old man and says "Well, it made a big difference to that one."

Just because we can't change everything shouldn't be an excuse to do nothing. There is always something you can do.

Do the Unexpected—"Be Like Water"

Humans are creatures of habit and convention. We take comfort in the familiar, and although we are capable of many diverse forms of behavior, a person's "repertoire" of behavior and reactions to a situation is usually the same and therefore predictable. This predictability becomes even stronger in industries, communities, or any environment where humans interact. The group exerts a collective peer pressure on one another that compels similar ways of thinking and therefore similar behavior. This is why Hannibal's approach to warfare was so effective against the Romans. In the ancient world there were certain protocols in battle that antagonists were expected to follow, but Hannibal tore up the rule book and as a result the Romans were totally out of their depth and at a loss as to how to deal with him. They were so enraged by his behavior that they even coined the phrase "Punic faith" to describe untrustworthy or dishonorable behavior. (Punic was the adjective to describe Carthage.) This is the same response that one would expect from an old English colonial gentleman blustering that his opponent's behavior was "just not cricket!"

This approach to competition is the single greatest lesson that Hannibal has to teach us today: Do the unthinkable. However, this is much easier said than done. We have to detach ourselves from the attitudes that very often we have grown up with, and think in a way that can feel totally alien to us. One of the best ways of expressing this fluid and creative way of thinking comes from the book *The Tao of Jeet Kun Do*, written by martial arts expert Bruce Lee. In it, he advises his students to "be like water." By this he means that rather than being rigid in our approach to life, we should be able to let our responses flow into a situation and react as required. The most impressive aspect of Hannibal's creativity was that he treated every situation differently and created his strategies to suit the environment he found himself in, rather than reverting to tired old ideas that he had used a hundred times before. Of course like many things in life this is easier said than done. So how can we take this approach and use it to make our own lives more effective? One of the ways that I have found works well is to remove myself from the mental environment of a particular industry or sport that I am immersed in, and read books about totally unrelated businesses, cultures, or whatever I find interests me. By doing this, I am attempting to get a different perspective on the situation that I am in. I am literally trying to acquire new thoughts and approaches that no one else within my industry has seen before. The management cliché term for this is "thinking outside the box," but although this term is somewhat over-used, that is exactly what Hannibal did. If Hannibal was a management guru today, this is what his key message would be. In the past you may not have realized the effectiveness of this approach, but now that you know the effect that Hannibal's "thinking outside the box" had on the Romans, you may want to apply it to your own field.

OK, so let's imagine that Hannibal was here to advise us today.

Remember that in Hannibal's case he was trapped in Spain, as the Romans had complete control of the seas. As we know, he not only decided to do the unthinkable by invading Italy, but incredibly, he did it by taking a whole army and elephants over the Alps.

Now think of a problem that you have been wrestling with for a while, either at work or in your personal life. What could you do that is as radical as Hannibal? What is the environment like? Can you use it as Hannibal did at Trebia? What are the personalities involved? If you are competing with them, can you use their personality traits against them as Hannibal did against both Sempronius and Fabius? Let your mind go wild and write all your ideas down on a piece of paper. Sometimes it is fun to imagine Hannibal sitting in front of you and pretend you are asking his advice. "Hannibal, I can't get this company to let me do a presentation. What would you do?" "Ride elephants through their head office!" If I have inspired you enough to look to the giants of history for advice, then you can pick your own favorites as your panel of advisers. What about Columbus, or Moses? Choose a character with the attributes you know would help solve your problem, and ask their advice. If you are willing to sit still, quiet your mind, and listen to what you think their answers might be, it is amazing the wisdom that this little game helps your imagination to release. If you have young children, ask their advice, as their answers are often unfettered by convention. What different routes could you take? Don't judge the ideas, just write them down. You can examine them later.

If you want other inspirations, think about when Hannibal duped the Romans into thinking the cattle were his army, or when he catapulted the snakes into the boats to win the sea battle. What different thought processes and methods could you apply to your problem that would leave those around you speechless? Incidentally, this is exactly the method that was used to win the Trojan War. Rather than waiting outside Troy for another ten years, they hid inside a wooden horse! Bizarre, but it worked.

Similar Behavior, Similar Results

Hannibal was once asked who he believed was the greatest general of all time. He answered "Alexander the Great." When I was studying the life and generalship of Hannibal, I was struck by the similarity between the two. It is very likely that Hannibal studied the life of Alexander and was very probably influenced by his actions. It makes me smile to think that someone as brilliant as Hannibal took inspiration from the giants of history in the same way that I do. This reveals another very powerful and timeless lesson: That similar actions produce similar results. Regardless of the time or place, people who act consistently tend to produce similar effects in their lives. History leaves us clues, and all we have to do is follow them. This is exactly the point I was making when I talked about learning from mentors and role models, and reading the lives of characters in history that you admire. Despite the advances in technology, life has not really changed that much. People are still animated by the same desires and passions. It is only the backdrop to our lives that has changed. Our hearts and minds are the same as those of our ancient ancestors. We are still animated by ambition and love, vulnerable to jealousies and fears. That is why the ancient religions and even the works of Shakespeare are still meaningful to us, as we relate to ourselves and each other in the same way the original audiences did. In the chapter on Alexander the Great, I talked about leading from the front, and how to earn the loyalty and respect of your staff or those around you. I could have written the same lesson in the chapter on Hannibal as well. I take great encouragement from this. I know that if I want to produce a result in my life, be it motivating myself or others, building a huge business or having courage in the face of overwhelming odds, one of the first things I do is find a series of characters who did the same thing. By reading about their lives, I learn that I am not alone in my challenges or desires, and that they all tended to act in a similar way. There really is no great mystery to it. They all had the same cognitive map, and all we have to do is follow it.

Use Your Competitors' Strength Against Them

To he who is good with a hammer, everything looks
like a nail.

Abraham Maslow

At the start of this chapter I said that we are creatures of habit.
We can use this predictability to our advantage. People, sports
teams, or companies who are very skilled in a certain area tend
to want to repeat that behavior over and over again. The
longer they do it, the harder it becomes for them to change.
They may not consciously decide to behave in this way, but
they will find it hard to behave otherwise. It is as if they are on
automatic pilot. They become very proud of and attached to
their skill, and as a result it becomes very difficult to change or
abandon it altogether. The irony is that this skill, if relied on
to excess, can actually become a vulnerability. At the battle of
Cannea, Hannibal used the weakness of the Gauls to defeat
the Romans, by using their infantry's superior discipline against
them. There are so many areas where this principle can be
applied today. Smaller companies can use a huge multinational's strength to defeat them if they can think creatively
to turn it to their advantage. So next time you are confronted
by a competitor who is vastly superior in a certain area and
wants to crush you, rather than being intimidated by it, think
like Hannibal, and see their strength as a chink in their armor
that will help you defeat them.

We know that Hannibal, despite his genius, was
ultimately defeated by the growing might of Rome. This part
of the story contains one of the saddest lessons, and was the
tragedy of Hannibal's life.

The Past Is Gone, You Cannot Recreate It

Hannibal was a general of the old school. His only wish was to recapture the days of his father and go back to the time when Carthage was a great commercial maritime power. As a result, his plan and vision lacked real purpose. Despite his military genius, his plan was naïve. It was as if he was still the young child at the altar trying to keep his promise to his father. The older we get the greater the temptation to yearn for the good old days. The irony is that the good old days were usually never that good, but given enough time, humans can romanticize almost anything. The problem with yearning for the past, be it in love or anything else, is that the very nature of yearning keeps us from focusing on the present and future. It mentally locks us into the past. This attitude prevents us from seeing and being grateful for the beauty and the gifts that our present contains. If for some reason our present situation is particularly bad, then yearning for the past will prevent us from tapping into the inner resources we need to make things better and so create a future for ourselves. The only really positive aspect of looking to our past is if our present is painful, and we want to change it. If we know that we contributed to the situation we are in at the moment, then looking at our past with as objective a view as possible can help us understand what we did to cause it. Very often our attitudes and behavior repeat the same situations in our lives. Unless we can see that and have the guts to change, we remain a victim of it. However, objectively analyzing what we did in the past and yearning for it are very different things. Our past can be viewed as the foundations that got us to where we are today, a source of lessons, gratitude and happiness, but to yearn for its return is point-less, futile, and ultimately can contribute nothing to our lives.

A Lesson from Fabius: If Your Opponent Is an Excellent Fighter . . . Don't Fight Him!

It is fascinating how history repeats itself with predictable regularity. Fabius knew that the correct way to defeat Hannibal was not to fight him, but to wear him down gradually by depriving him of supplies, but his plan was over-thrown by those who could not bear to see their lands being destroyed. Years earlier, the mercenary leader Memnon had urged King Darius to do the same thing to Alexander the Great, but his plan too was abandoned, for the same reason. Both plans, if implemented, would have been disastrous for the two great generals. Fabius was actually demonstrating the same creative logic that Hannibal applied to his own strategies. His apparent passivity was in fact to Hannibal the most lethal form of aggression. When a competitor is highly skilled in a certain area, they will always try to make you compete with them in that skill. However, if possible, it is much wiser to change the rules of the game and so nullify their strength in that area. If your competitor is excellent at football, make him play rugby; if a company has a great sales force, compete on the Internet. It is up to you to try and see how you can choose where the battle is fought, but if you can, avoid at all costs going head-to-head with them at the one thing that they are brilliant at. Even if you win, you will still come away bloody.

A Lesson from Scipio Africanus: Imitation Is the Highest Form of Flattery

Scipio idolized Hannibal, and ironically it was this intense admiration that ultimately defeated him. By watching him intently throughout his campaign in Italy, Scipio became Hannibal's most eager student, studying his every move and method. We can learn so much from Scipio's humility and willingness to learn from a man who was effectively destroying his country and society. Very often, when we are confronted by an individual, team, or company who is obviously superior in any given area, the temptation is to try and play down their abilities or to complain about them to our friends. It takes a very confident and humble person to be able to admit that they are totally outclassed for the moment, and to be willing to learn from their competitor. However, by doing this and biding your time, you begin to see that no individual is infallible, and when the time comes, you will have your Zama.

Scipio also sends a message of warning to all competitors who are complacent in their superiority, and that is: Be wary of competing with the same opponent repeatedly, as no matter how good you think you are, they will eventually work out how you do it and play you at your own game.

When I began to study the story of Hannibal, my intention had been to use him as an excellent example of creative strategies and outwitting opponents. However, once I became immersed in his story, the most powerful lessons I learned were not from Hannibal, but from the Roman Republic.

Failure Is Not an Option

A quote that sums up this lesson is from the *Star Wars* character, Yoda, when he says to a reluctant Luke Skywalker, "There is do and do not. There is no try." The word try is such a cop-out, it's like a "get-out-of-jail free" card. When discussing a matter of real importance that somebody says they will try to do, they are just building-in the excuse that they will use later when they have not succeeded. "Well I only said I would *try*." Of course there is always the chance of failure, but the fear of it should never put us off from starting a project: It is imperative that we do not start off with that option in mind.

Our ancestors never had the option of "trying" to do something, as so many of their actions were motivated by simple survival. Due to their success and sacrifices, we in the developed world now enjoy incredible levels of abundance, and this luxury has made us emotionally flabby. We can "try" to succeed in our careers and the various other projects we tinker with, as the consequences of failure are rarely terminal. This is the opposite attitude to that which animates the actions of the indigenous people that I have worked with in the developing world when I have been on expedition. The Bedouins of Sinai don't "try" to find water, and the tribesmen of Kashmir don't "try" to catch their prey when they are hunting, and the women don't "try" to prepare for winter. The consequences of failure for these people are very often fatal. This self-reliant attitude reveals itself in the way they walk, talk, and treat everyone they meet. There is a complete lack of ego and pretension in their bearing. The one aspect of their behavior that has struck me repeatedly on my trips has been that they never complain about how hard their life is. Ironically, they appear to be a lot more content and satisfied with their lives than many of us in the West. This is because they know who they are, and what they are capable of, and have a deep respect for themselves and the other people in their communities.

This is the gift we bestow upon ourselves when we mentally decide to stop making excuses and give our all, to our lives, and the lives of the people we love. It is amazing how much stronger and more determined you become when you remove the option of failing from your mind. It takes courage and mental and emotional stamina, but that attitude results in a steely resolve that is hard to beat and has a powerfully intimidating effect on your would-be competitors.

When it comes to the things that really matter, we instinctively know that "trying" is not an option. The mother whose daughter is trapped in a burning car does not "try" to save her. This is the emotional and mental state that we have to bring to the aspects of our lives that are deeply important to us: That we will simply give it everything we have got and will never give up until we have succeeded. But if it is so apparent that removing the option of failure is extra-ordinarily powerful in terms of achieving what is important to us, why then doesn't everyone do it? Why do we see so many projects fail because of half-hearted attempts? The reason is that many of us fear that if we really give our all, and it still does not work, then we will expose ourselves to the pain of defeat and the ridicule of others. This is true as much in love as it is in business or sport. The irony is that the fear of failure causes hesitancy and that hesitancy causes our worst fears to come true. Furthermore, if we give something our all, not only are the chances of succeeding massively increased, but also that if, despite our best efforts, things still don't work out, it actually makes the disappointment easier to take. We still have our precious self-respect and are free from the nagging guilt that we know deep down we really could have done better. Another benefit of mentally removing the option of failure and allowing yourself to give your all, is that the people around you will see it in you and respect you for it. We see this in sport all the time. A competitor runs themself into the ground, but despite being defeated, is given a standing ovation by the crowd. Giving your all is an excellent reputation to develop.

Many of us go through life trying to do as little as possible to get by, but when we look at the implications of this behavior in our future we are presented with another brutal truth:

If You Do Not Choose to Pay the Price for Success,
You Will Pay the Price for Failure

By doing nothing, failure creeps up on you. We often forget that as we sow, we reap. The actions we take in life culminate in momentums that lead us down the road that we have chosen either consciously or by accident. It cracks me up when I see people who do the absolute minimum at work, spend their evenings in the pub, and constantly avoid doing anything that is remotely uncomfortable to them, then years later complain that they are broke, overweight, and have done nothing with their lives. What did they expect? That was the life they chose. Now if they live a life like that and it makes them happy and they are aware of the consequences, then great, they have lived what was for them a successful life. I do not buy into the concept of success and failure as black and white, and I would never dream of calling someone a failure as it denies the inherent dignity of a person's humanity. I define success and failure as simply whether you have managed to create the life you want to lead. If you are constantly dissatisfied and yearning for something but not doing anything about it, then that is what I would define as failure. But if you are living the life you want to live no matter what that is, then I define that as success. It's a deeply personal thing. Another interesting thing is that if somebody endeavors to succeed at a goal but fails, when they look back at their life they know that they gave it their best shot. They did their utmost, and that is all that can be asked of anyone. It is a dangerous delusion to believe that avoiding the effort to succeed at something will have no consequences. By choosing to avoid the effort necessary to create the life we want, whatever that life may be, we inadvertently choose to fail, and there is no one to blame but ourselves. So consider the consequences of your inaction.

The Romans endured horrific loss of life at the hands of Hannibal and seemed helpless to be able to do anything to stop him. They could have chosen a hundred times to give in and sue for peace but they would not countenance it. It simply was not an option. It is no surprise that they went on to create the Roman Empire. Such courage and deter-mination is unstoppable. Now pause and consider for a second: What would have been the implications if they had given in? How different would the world be today? There would never have been "the glory that was Rome." There would have been no Emperor Constantine to convert the

Roman Empire to Christianity and help it spread and ultimately become a world religion. There would have been no interaction of western European cultures, no Renaissance. The list could go on for ever, as the influence of Rome is so much a part of who we are. Closer to home, what would have happened if the British had decided in their darkest hour that resisting Hitler was too difficult and signed a treaty ending the war and allowing him to dominate Europe?

The only reason that we can see the wisdom of the Romans or the courage of the British is because we are looking back at them from the distance of time, but when they were going through their tests, they did not have the luxury of knowing that they would ultimately prevail, that they would come out the other side.

Now I know that these are world-changing events, but this principle applies as much to our own lives. Is there or has there ever been a period in your life when you were being tested to breaking point and you felt that you were going to give up? Now ask yourself what would have been the implications for your future if you had. To use a business example, every single one of the people I know who have become extremely successful in business went through periods in their lives when they were seriously tempted to give in and walk away from their dreams and goals. They all held on despite the odds and now enjoy the fruits of their success. Now when they look back and think of everything they would have lost if they had given in, they shudder at how different their lives would have been.

It amazes me when I see the jealousy and resentment that some people feel at other people's success. Yes, there are a few who win the lottery, but in business, sport, or other endeavors the vast majority of those who win did so because they overcame the challenges that life put in their path. It i always revealing to talk to a successful person in any field. We tend to see only the finished article and not the scared and exhausted person they were when they first started and were struggling against the odds. We only see the football sta scoring the touchdown to win the game and not the years of grueling training they had endured to get there. Real success in any walk of life is never an accident. You may think you want something, but the challenges are there to make sure you really do. And believe me, every reason I have ever heard for giving in has been experienced by someone who kept going and won. I am not blaming people for giving in. know how hard trying to achieve a dream can be. It's just that if the person who gave in could look back at their life from the perspective of the tenacity of the Romans and see what they could have done and the person they could have become if only they had kept going, it would probably break their heart.

Now you may be sitting there saying, "Yeah that's easier said than done." Believe me, I know. There have been times when I could not sleep as I sweated blood thinking that I was three months away from bankruptcy. On K2 I knew I was dying, and that the man I was trying to save was dying too but I had to keep going, carrying him on my back. But please don't think I am lecturing you. Rather than telling you what you should do, I am going to suggest some things that can help you acquire the resolve to face the challenging periods in your life. These are some imaginary devices that I developed to help me keep going. Again, trust me, they work.

Use Your Imagination to Create Instant Hindsight

Life can only be understood backwards but it has to
be lived forwards.

Søren Kierkegaard

When we are in the middle of a difficult time in our lives it
helps to get some perspective and to look at the situation
from a distance in much the same way that we look at history.
It is said that we are always wiser with hindsight. In many
cases, deep down we already know what we should do in a
challenging situation. If we allow ourselves to listen to our
innermost feelings, that wisdom can be revealed. One
method that can help to clarify those thoughts is to use our
imaginations to create hindsight artificially.

Sit back, relax, close your eyes, and once you have calmed
your mind, imagine drifting five to ten years into the future.
In this imaginary future picture yourself having achieved all
the things you would like to happen, and that the challenging situation you are going through has been resolved to
the best for everyone concerned.

Now picture yourself as you are in the future—happy and
confident because this situation is a distant memory and
everything has worked out perfectly.

Once you have that image in your mind, ask the older
you to advise you on what you should do now to resolve the
situation, and then simply listen to the answers.

It is amazing how simply getting some perspective on
our problems can make us feel a lot better about them.
They don't seem so big, so overwhelming. This imaginary
exercise also allows us to tap into the vast resources of

wisdom that are buried inside all of us and get some clarity.

Another technique you can employ is to imagine a light, like a huge lighthouse, illuminating your whole life in the present and the future. This psychologically removes the areas of darkness and doubt in our lives that we are unsure of and can help us to find the right path.

Even if your life is going really well, these mental processes are very effective at clarifying what you want to achieve in your life and at helping you to understand whether the path you are currently taking is leading you where you want to go.

It is very helpful to read as many stories as you can about people who overcame similar challenges. This is what we talked about in the chapter on Alexander the Great, when we discussed learning from role models and using books to form cognitive maps.

I want to stress again that while it is very easy to say, "when things are tough, never give up," it is much harder to do in real life. The above techniques can help you to actually develop the faith and mental stamina to keep going. I have observed again and again that in areas as diverse as business and mountaineering, the difference between those who give up and those who keep going is solely down to how they process what they are experiencing in their imaginations.

There are so many things that you can achieve, so much that you can give to the world, so many people you will be able to help, but none of it will come to pass, and you will go to your grave with your music still in you, if you give in when you are tested. So when your trials seem unbearable and it seems that there is no way out, think of the guts and determination of the young Roman Republic, and remember, one victory does not win a war, so face your defeats with fortitude and never, ever give in.

However, there is one exception to this advice that the Romans in Hannibal's story teach us.

If What You Are Doing Isn't Working, Stop Doing It!

The Romans were massacred at Cannea, despite their massive numerical superiority, because they kept attacking Hannibal in the same ineffective way and as a result he knew exactly how to defeat them. They had developed a way of fighting battles that had worked for them in the past and as a result they simply repeated the same methods over and over. Very often when somebody fails repeatedly despite their best efforts they are tempted to give in due to the intense frustration and despair it engenders. It is at this darkest hour that it is important we remind ourselves that mistakes are not meant to be repeated; they are meant to be learned from.

If you are clear in your mind that you are passionately committed to achieving a goal and willing to do the work necessary to achieve it, then you will almost definitely encounter the problem that your first efforts will not always produce the success you believed they would. It is at this point that most people are tempted to give in. It is at this point that they are most vulnerable. But what most of us don't know is that making mistakes is an essential part of the process of achieving our goals. Thankfully the implications of failure are not as horrific for most of us as they were for the Romans after the defeats that they suffered at the hands of Hannibal. Despite the fact that the stakes are much smaller, the principles involved are the same. Mistakes and defeats are inevitable, and if you are mentally prepared to accept this then you will not feel indignant, resentful, or crushed when they occur. If you really accept the fact that failure is not terminal, then you can actually become quite excited about it, as you realize that every mistake is actually taking you closer to your goal. This is not some patronizing motivational nonsense, but a real approach that I have observed in many of my peers. Their response to failure seems to be "Good, so now I know that that approach does not work, it will help me find the one that does." Where the people who give up and those who learn from their defeats differ is that the ones who keep going take a step back and study why they were not successful from every possible angle. They read books, ask other people's advice, find out why they were not successful, and then change their approach.

This is exactly what the Romans did. The reason they were successful in the end was because they finally changed their approach and learned how to play Hannibal at his own game. If they had not and had kept on marching to their doom in the same formation, all the determination and courage in the world would not have saved them from extinction. They had to take all their admirable courage and determination and channel it in a different direction. A great piece of advice that sums this approach up is "Carve your goals in stone and your plans in sand." Your ultimate goal is precious and should not be abandoned easily, but you should be able to change your plans as often as is necessary at a moment's notice.

One of my mentors that I mentioned in chapter one lost $53,000 in the first three months of his first business and went bust. Rather than despairing, he picked himself up and went on to form three very successful businesses in succession. On the other hand, I know other people whose first failure in a given field caused them such despair that they never tried again. They were not any weaker or less talented than him but they interpreted the lack of initial success in a way that prevented them from tapping into their inner resources and trying again. In chapter one we looked at this area in the self-image section, but I would like to refine the concept further by looking at what I call our personal creation myth.

Construct Your Personal Creation Myth

One of mankind's most basic psychological needs is the need to create meaning: The need to make sense of our environment and the events that take place in our lives. A recurring theme throughout this book is that it is not so much what happens to us in our lives that matters, but rather how we respond and react to what happens to us. The key determinant of how we react to a given situation is the meaning that we attach to that event. One of the main ways in which humans create meaning to help them to understand themselves, the world, and their place in it, is by telling stories. And the most significant and revealing story in any culture is its creation myth.

If you look at every ancient culture, you will see that they all have a story, usually fantastical, of where they came from. The Mongols believed that a "blue wolf took as his mate a fallow doe" and that their offspring were the tribe of the Mongols. Romans believed that the founders of Rome were the brothers Romulus and Remus, who were raised by a she-wolf. One of ancient Rome's most powerful images is that of the infant boys being suckled by the she-wolf like two cubs. (We will see why this image is so powerful later in this chapter.) In the West, the spread of Christianity has meant that the ancient Celtic and pagan creation myths are not widely known, and they have been replaced by the story of Adam and Eve, and God creating the world in seven days.

But creation myths are not passive fantasies. They form an integral part of our identity and our conception of who we are as a culture, a race, and a nation. One of the most important lessons from Hannibal's story is how the Romans refused to give in, how tough and unyielding they were in the face of horrendous defeats. Why was this? Well, perhaps one reason is the fact that they believed that they were descended from children who had a wolf for a mother. This general toughness and harsh attitude to life further revealed itself in the sports they enjoyed. Gladiatorial games were popular because the Romans actually believed that compassion was a vice and a weakness. This revealing insight into the collective self-image of the Romans helps us understand why they reacted the way they did to the threat of Hannibal. They did not roll over and give in because that was simply not who they were, and people always act in line with their identities.

Important stories in a culture's collective identity are often romanticized accounts of the great trials and tests that they endured. Every culture has them, but interestingly, people only remember or promote the stories that reinforce the attributes and behaviors they believe in. The stories of a country's finest hour are an attempt to preserve their best selves in an attempt to encourage that behavior. In the story of Hannibal, the tales of the Roman people rallying to help the legionnaires as they marched to defeat the army of Hasdrubal (and so ultimately force Hannibal to return to Carthage) became an essential part of their national identity and a symbol of their ability to stand together against the odds and so turn the tide.

Here are some other examples: The Americans have mythologized the battle of the Alamo, where a group of colorful individuals made a last stand against the Mexican army. This image of rugged individuals standing together to fight for their freedom resonates very deeply with the American psyche. The Scots venerate the campaigns of William Wallace, the guerrilla freedom fighter who was eventually brutally executed by the English. However, cultures are very selective in the stories they choose to remember. To use another Scottish example, ask anyone in Scotland if they have heard of the battle of Bannockburn, and they will tell you that it is where Robert the Bruce and his tiny army defeated the English and thus won their freedom. The Scots sing songs about it at soccer matches, and we have images of it on our banknotes. It is a part of populist culture, as it fits in with the Scottish identity of a small nation bravely overcoming the tyranny of their larger neighbor. However, if you ask the Scots if they have ever heard of the battle of Flodden, most of them will say no. This is because this was when the Scots sneakily tried to invade England when her back was turned and the English in their own fit of heroics totally annihilated the Scots, killing their king and half the Scottish nobility in the process. It's no surprise that Flodden is not taught in Scottish schools.

This is not a purely Scottish phenomenon. While on

expedition on K2, I was chatting with some French climbers about European history and mentioned the battle of Agincourt—made famous by Shakespeare—when the English longbowmen decimated the vastly superior French knights. None of them had ever heard of it and they were none too pleased when I told them the story. They then proceeded to list the spectacular victories of Napoleon, but became annoyed when I mentioned Waterloo. The point I am making is that countries and cultures celebrate their victories in songs and monuments and name places after them. Why do you think in London we have Waterloo station and Trafalgar Square?

So why am I telling you all this? How does this phenomenon help us in our lives?

Haven't you noticed that most people seem to know every embarrassing event in their past off by heart: Who was there, what happened, how they felt? They also know all their supposed failures and their bad points, and as a result all the reasons why they cannot succeed. This is the psychological equivalent of hanging symbols of all your mistakes around your neck. If these people were to build towns they would even name places after them. Can you imagine that? "Yeah, just go down 'Can't Get a Girlfriend Street,' turn left into 'Failed My Maths Exam Place,' and you'll be in 'First Business Went Bust Square.'" Why is it that as cultures we celebrate our successes and the things and events we are most proud of, but as individuals this is seen as crass, egoistic, and vain? How did it become desirable or acceptable to put ourselves down? Think about it: If our friends put us down the way we put ourselves down, we wouldn't stay friends with them for very long.

So starting right now, let's decide that we will take the same approach to our own identities that entire cultures take to theirs. We will remember, enhance, and celebrate the events that we are most proud of and put all the memories of the events that hold us back and make us miserable in the dark. We will be the French climbers who had never heard of Agincourt or the Scots who don't think about the defeat at Flodden. You might think it's delusional to remember only the good things and forget about the things we don't want to remember, but if whole countries can do it, why can't you? I am not saying deny events ever happened, but rather don't wear them like millstones round your neck and let them hold you back or dominate your whole concept of who you are. Nor am I saying that we are going to become ignorant or emotionally one-dimensional, as we can learn a lot and grow from our mistakes. No, all I am trying to do is to get some balance, to encourage you to give yourself a break and remember all the things you have done that make you happy, empowered, and confident. Rehashing painful memories and playing them over and over in your mind serves no purpose whatsoever. It's time we broke that habit.

So let's do something about it right now, rather than just talking about it. Think of a memory that makes you feel uncomfortable. Don't pick something that was particularly traumatic, but rather something that is more in line with failing a minor exam at school. What we are going to do works with the more painful memories, but let's demonstrate it with the less painful things first.

- Take the memory and create an image of it in your mind's eye. Got it? How does that make you feel?

- Now imagine your mind is a TV screen. If the memory is moving, make it static.
- If there is noise in this memory, turn the sound off.
- Turn the image from color to black and white.
- Now imagine that you are playing with the reception and make the image go all blurry and faint.
- Next pretend that you have a zoom lens and push the image as far away from you as possible until it is just a little dot in the distance, then make it disappear. It's fun if you make a little "pop" noise when you do this.

If you did that little process properly, you should have noticed that as you made the image smaller and more distant the uncomfortable feelings lessened in intensity also. Do you see the power of what you just did? By changing the way your mind represented a memory, you took control of the way it made you feel. This demonstrates that it is not the memory of events that makes us feel bad, but rather the way we represent them to ourselves. Of course, more painful memories take a bit more effort to dislodge but the principle is the same.

Next take an image of something that you are particularly proud of. Perhaps if you picked a memory of you failing an exam in the last process, you could pick one of you passing one brilliantly to replace it with. If you are having trouble finding a spectacular success, then scour your memory for something you did that could be considered a success, no matter how small. This is not the time to judge yourself.

This time we are going to do the exact opposite.

- Take that memory and make the colors as bright as you can; turn up the definition.

- If there is no sound, turn it up and make the sounds clear and resonant.
- Now bring the image closer to you, and closer still.
- Once the image is as close, as clear and as bright as you can make it, actually step into the memory and relive it as if it was happening again.

I bet that made you feel better. Really enjoy all those great feelings again.

Can you imagine the effect this could have on your day-to-day life? Believe me, it massively increases the chances of you recreating your successes again and again. Your memories are yours, so isn't it time you turned them into your best allies? They are not random occurrences in your brain; you control them. Incidentally, if you want to make yourself feel really bad, just dredge up your painful memories and put them through the second process. That is exactly what we do to ourselves when we are miserable: we are reliving the experiences that hurt us by stepping into them.

Now let's take the concept of creation myth even further to create a more resilient, resourceful, and powerful concept of who we are.

Earlier we discussed how creation myths are fantastical stories that explain how a tribe, race, or society came into existence, and how the stories that cultures choose to remember are selective memories that portray the attributes they admire, wish to be associated with, and nurture in themselves. Now we are going to do exactly the same thing for ourselves.

Sit back and think of an attribute or trait that you would like to have more of. This time you can think of a time when you acted with particular confidence, courage, etc. Once you have thought of this event, put it through the second process I just showed you. By reliving various memories of you when you were confident and in control, you actually help to make that attribute grow in you.

Now let's take this process one step further.

- Close your eyes and think of an attribute or form of behavior that you would like to be able to have but have real difficulty with, or believe that you have never demonstrated in your life.
- Now imagine someone whose behavior epitomizes the trait that you would like to acquire, and picture that character displaying the trait, with absolute ease.
- As you are watching them in your mind's eye, ask yourself what they would need to believe about life and themselves in order to act like that. Listen to the answers that come to you.
- Imagine what those beliefs would feel like, and as you do so, bring the image of their behavior closer and make it brighter, bolder, and clearer.
- Try to imagine and intensify the type of feelings that this character must be feeling in order to act like that.
- When you have made the image as bright and as close and as powerful as you can, step into the body of the character in your mind and see yourself carrying out that behavior.
- Watch yourself behaving like this over and over. Once you are familiar with this image, tell yourself that this is one of your own memories.

Yes, exactly: You are going to artificially create memories of yourself acting in the way that demonstrates the traits you want to acquire. This may seem a little unusual and strange to you at first, but think about it. In chapter one we looked at how our memories of our abilities affect our self-image. Here we are constructing memories of the traits of the attributes you desire. By doing this over and over you will be able to remember various clear memories of you being confident at interviews, or whatever you have decided upon. This is no different from a golfer practicing perfect golf swings in his imagination. You are practicing new behaviors, and by imagining that you have already behaved like that in the past, your mind will find it much easier to accept them as part of you.

Many of the memories from our past that confirm either positive or negative beliefs we have about ourselves, the world or other people are inaccurate. Our memories by their very nature are subjective and convey solely our own impression of the event. Have you ever discussed a past event with some-body who was there also and you both totally disagree on key facts of what happened? Very often our memories degrade and change with time, yet we treat as unassailable fact those memories that support the aspects of our self-perception that we are most attached to, and these often inaccurate memories construct our idea of who we are. Of course I am not saying that you have to actually believe your artificially created memories. If you say to people, "Yes, that reminds me of the time I won the Grand Prix" you will soon get a reputation. But by imagining these constructed memories as already having happened, the new behavior will seem natural to you, and you will be able to adopt it as part of you more gracefully.

There is one other key thing that societies and cultures

do when remembering their victories and triumphs. They build monuments to them. Go to any major city or town in any country in the world and you will get an instant insight into the actions and behaviors that the inhabitants are most proud of by the monuments that they have erected to commemorate them. By building a monument, the inhabitants are attempting to relive the feeling of pride, victory, or whatever emotion the event symbolized to them.

Again we can take inspiration from this and use our imaginations to create a stronger, more powerful sense of self-worth. Remember, the difference between someone who cracks under pressure and someone who endures is that the latter has a stronger sense of who they are, what they are capable of, and a greater belief that they will prevail. It is this inner resource that they draw on for the courage and faith to keep going, and its source is their memories and imaginations. Now we are going to take this idea and use it to strengthen our concept of who we are.

Build a Museum to Your Triumphs

In your imagination, imagine a place where you feel most at ease. It can be anywhere you want, be it a temple, castle, forest, or mountaintop. Now cast your mind back to your earliest memory of doing something that you are proud of, and place a memorial to that event in the place you have chosen. Place this symbol at one end of the scene.

Continue to remember as many things as you can, right up to the present day. Each time you create a new monument or symbol, place it next to the previous one, so that you can imagine yourself walking along looking at them as if you are walking from your past to the present day. It can help to place a date next to the event.

When you have finished, your mind should have, say, a huge mountaintop temple filled with images of you scoring goals, winning awards, the birth of your children, even making people laugh. It is important to bring the scene to life so that the monuments really communicate the treasured emotions that those achievements created in you. By strolling along this museum, you can powerfully remind yourself of all the things you have actually achieved in your life and maybe taken for granted. This imaginary technique helps to create not only a buoyant positive self-image, but also a positive self-expectancy as to what our future holds for us. Here's how you do it.

Again in your imagination, walk along the rows of your monuments until you reach the present day. Then imagine the things that you want to achieve in the future and create wonderful monuments to them and a date beside them. Keep walking along, looking at all the wonderful things that your future holds for you, but make sure you tell yourself that you are actually looking at monuments to achievements that have already occurred. This belief that you have already achieved your goals has a very powerful subconscious effect and actually helps to create the inner resources you need to go after them and make them true. You can have great fun with this. When you achieve a new goal, imagine a procession carrying your new monument into your victory place. This mental rehearsal makes commuting on the train a lot more entertaining, and it *really* works.

Incidentally, if you are having trouble accepting that these imaginary devices can actually create a change in your emotions, answer this question. When you are scared or nervous before a first date, a competition, or a job interview what creates the fear? The answer? Your imagination. Even if you are not consciously imagining fearful images, your subconscious is picturing them below the surface. When a child is scared of monsters under the bed it is their imagination that is torturing them. Adults smile at the silliness of childish fears but ironically put themselves through exactly the same process when they believe that they can't take a chance in their life because of all the things they imagine will go wrong. By taking control of our imagination, we tackle our emotions at the source rather than being victims of them by believing they are produced by random chance. Repeating these mental processes increases their power and influence. Our minds are like gardens: What we sow in them we reap.

Now that you are familiar with the concept of how people tell themselves romanticized stories of where they came from and who they are, you will begin to notice it in other people and be able to see how it helps them to form their identity. I remember watching an interview with Donald Trump, the American real-estate tycoon. He was asked about his parents and quick as a flash volunteered the information that "My mother was a MacLeod. They were a clan of warriors." This statement reveals that the romantic history of the warlike Scottish clans he was descended from was an important part of his identity. The MacLeods have not fought as a cohesive clan unit for centuries, but that memory of his ancestors appeared to be very precious to him and he chose to build an emotional bond with their image. By associating with this clan and imagining the traits they must have exhibited, such as courage and determination, he enhanced those traits in himself. He also focused on the trait that he related to or wanted to enhance in himself. He did not mention that the majority of the MacLeods were poor and were defeated in various battles. Creation myths are not affected by exact historical accuracy but rather by the emotional effect they have on the listeners. Remember, Alexander the Great believed he was descended from Hercules and Achilles, and you know the effect his creation myth had on his self-image and behavior. Donald Trump's statement is an excellent example of an individual's personal creation myth.

What is your family's creation myth, your sports team's, your company's? What are your proudest moments? If you are the coach or captain of a football team you can recreate the time when you came back at half-time from four goals down to win the game, and use it as a powerful emotive image to inspire the team to fight back when they are being beaten. Families can remember the times they pulled together when a parent was made redundant or suffered illness. Creation myths remind us of who we are, and why we are that way. They form our identity and our identities create self-fulfilling prophecies. If your memory is full of your victories it is very hard for you to accept defeat, and as a result, like the Romans, you will keep going despite the odds and ultimately prevail. If you choose to remember all your defeats—and let's face it, we all have plenty of them—then the minute you suffer a minor setback your mind will say, "Here we go again." So take control of the memories you choose to focus on, as they literally form your identity, which creates your behavior, your actions, and so ultimately, the kind of life you will lead. Construct a creation myth that tells you why you will win and will give you the courage to keep going.

Hannibal was defeated by the Romans and ultimately took his own life. That could be perceived as the ultimate defeat, but he taught us to hold fast to who we are and to fight for what we believe in despite the odds; that even in defeat, a legacy of honor, brilliance and bravery will outlive the setbacks we suffer during our lives. This is a lesson that our next character, who enjoyed the fruits of total victory throughout his life, would have done well to remember. The master spin doctor and original PR guru whose manipulation of the facts offends our concept of truth and justice. It is time we met William the Conqueror.

4

William the Conqueror

The Master of Perception

The grim-faced warlord scanned the shoreline, looking for the Anglo-Saxon army that he was sure would be waiting for him, but the beaches were empty. His forces would be allowed to land in peace. His heart raced as his boat crashed on to the beach. Soon he would set foot in England, the land whose throne he had come to claim. Wanting to be the first ashore, he made his way to the front of the boat and steadied himself to jump. His men roared behind him as he ran and leapt . . . and landed flat on his face in the sand.

The roar died in the throats of his men. Silence but for lapping waves gripped the beach. They stared in disbelief at their leader lying sprawled in the sand. To the devout Norman soldiers, this bad omen could only mean that God did not want them to invade England. They began to murmur that they should sail home immediately. On the shore the warlord's mind was racing. He had seconds to save the invasion campaign that had taken years to prepare. Spitting the sand from his mouth, he clambered to his feet and turned to face his frightened men. Raising his fists full of sand into the air he screamed "See, men, I have seized England with both hands already!"

The men cheered in relief and piled off the ships. The year was 1066, and the invasion of England had started. William of Normandy, the original master of spin, had arrived.

Beginnings—Medieval Double Dealings

The Norman invasion of England is one of the most traumatic events in English history. The battle of Hastings is ingrained in the psyche of the English people as the confrontation that resulted in the destruction of the Anglo-Saxon ruling class, and replaced it with Norman overlords and their way of life imported from France. Overnight the Anglo-Saxon population became the underclass in their own land. But what appeared to be a clash of cultures was actually a contest for supremacy between two men: William, Duke of Normandy, known to his friends as William the Bastard; and his archrival, Harold Godwinsson, the newly crowned King of England.

But how did a Norman duke think that he had a legitimate claim to the throne of England greater than that of an English nobleman? His claim was the result of a bizarre series of misunderstandings, twists of fate and double-dealings, many of which were orchestrated by William himself. Years before his troops even set foot in England, William had launched one of history's best PR campaigns, one that would make today's spin doctors proud.

It all began during the reign of the previous king of England, Edward the Confessor. Despite being an Anglo-Saxon, King Edward had gone to Normandy as a child and lived there for thirty years. While he was there, he had watched the young William grow up and survive repeated assassination attempts to become the steely Duke of Normandy, a title he had inherited at the vulnerable age of eight. Edward in his turn had survived the carnage that followed the death of King Canute, his predecessor. Canute had left no heir and the nobles of England had thrashed it out to claim the throne. Edward, a descendant of Alfred the Great, was the last man standing, but despite the fact that he had survived the carnage caused by the issue of succession, he also inherited a bitter thorn in his side: The mighty Godwin family, with the rapaciously ambitious Godwin, Earl of Wessex, at their head.

The Godwins were the real power behind Canute's throne, and Earl Godwin was determined to strengthen his grip during the reign of Edward, but there was one problem—Edward detested him. Earl Godwin had arranged the brutal murder of Edward's older brother during the succession wrangles, and Edward was determined to be rid of him and his power-hungry family. However, despite his best efforts at removing the Godwins (including deporting the Earl and appointing Norman lords in his place), their power grew stronger and Edward had to swallow the humiliation of being forced to marry Edith, Earl Godwin's daughter, so that she could provide a Godwin heir to the throne.

However, if we believe William of Normandy's PR machine, Edward did have the last laugh, and revenge against the Godwins. Although forced to marry Edith, he refused to consummate the marriage and turned to religion instead, earning himself the title Edward the Confessor. As a result he died childless, leaving no Godwin heir. Furthermore, according to William, Edward had secretly left the throne of England to him in order to spite the Godwins further. But the Godwins were not that easy to outwit, and they claimed that on his deathbed Edward had reached out and touched the hand of Harold, the eldest son and golden boy of the Godwin clan. Touched, but infuriatingly said nothing. The succession to the throne of England was again left open to speculation and doubt.

This is where the story could have ended, with Harold claiming that Edward had touched him and left him the crown and William protesting that, no, Edward had promised the throne to him. That is, if it weren't for the fickle hand of fate and William of Normandy's formidable talent for PR and spin.

Of All the Luck!

Harold Godwinsson is remembered as being a dashing and heroic figure. He had everything going for him, and with the power of the Godwins behind him it seemed as if his succession to the throne of England was a certainty. But unfortunately for him and the future of the English, he wasn't exactly the luckiest guy on the planet.

The first piece of bad luck in the saga occurred when Harold set sail across the Channel in 1064. Later on, William would promote the myth that Harold had sailed to Normandy in order to affirm Edward the Confessor's offer to the Duke of the crown of England, but maybe the real reason Harold made the journey was to rescue his younger brother,

Wolfstan, whom William just happened to be holding hostage.

Unfortunately for Harold, something went wrong during the journey and he was forced to land in the territory of a Norman nobleman loyal to none other than William of Normandy himself. In keeping with feudal law of the time, Harold and his companions were immediately handed over to William as his prisoners.

However, rather than throwing Harold into prison, William acted the perfect host, providing him with every comfort and even taking him on campaign with him, where Harold demonstrated his formidable bravery, an attribute that William would later encounter face-to-face. Whereas Harold behaved with his characteristic nobility towards his host, William, now that he had Harold in his clutches, orchestrated an exquisite emotional trap designed to ensnare Harold's conscience. It unfolded in three stages.

STAGE ONE

To cement their new friendship, William decided to make Harold a knight of Normandy. This meant that by law he was bound to protect Harold, but, as William was well aware, the promise went both ways and Harold also had to swear an oath of allegiance to William. Later William would insist that Harold had sworn to help him with his claim to the throne of England once Edward was dead.

STAGE TWO

Not only did William make Harold swear an oath, but he made the oath sacred by making Harold swear it in church.

STAGE THREE

Once Harold had made his oath, the cloth that covered the table upon which he had made it was pulled away to reveal a box containing holy relics and the bones of a saint!

"So what?" you say. Well, in medieval times, *nobody* went back on an oath, and to break one sworn over relics would send you straight to hell. In one smart move, William had raised the stakes involved in the struggle for the throne from simple power politics to Harold's very soul. Or at least that was what William said.

Harold's second piece of bad luck came from the unlikeliest of sources, within his own family. His younger brother, Tostig, the Earl of Northumbria, was a spoiled brat and his behavior was so unreasonable that he had single-handedly managed to cause a rebellion of the northern earls. King Edward sent Harold to try and calm the rebellion, but this presented him with a serious dilemma. Who should he support, the northern nobles or his brother? In order to prevent the rebellion spreading further, Harold did the right thing and backed the nobles, thus sending his brother into exile. As we will see later in the story, this decision would prove to be fatal for Harold and for England.

All Hail, Harold . . . King of England?

In the winter of 1065 Edward the Confessor died, and Harold, believing that he had been given the throne when Edward touched him on his deathbed, promptly declared himself king. In Normandy, William went berserk. He called assembly after assembly, insisting to his lords and knights that he had been betrayed and beseeching them to follow him on a campaign to England so that he could claim his throne. But there were no takers. It was simply too daring a plan for a duke to confront a king in his own country. Despite William's promise of land and riches for all, they simply were not willing to risk everything they had to help him claim a crown that only he believed was his.

What was William to do, give up? He had been telling everyone that he would soon be King of England, and he could imagine them sniggering behind his back. But William was not so easily defeated. Demonstrating a brilliant under-standing of the warped piety of the medieval mind, he decided to reframe his campaign in the minds of the followers he needed. In an act of blatant PR manipulation and shameless spin, he changed the campaign from one of simple greed and dynastic succession to a holy crusade against the godless heathen and sacred-oath-breaker Harold Godwinsson. He went straight to the Pope and made his best impassioned sales pitch. The Pope loved it. In fact he loved it so much that he gave William not only his blessing, but his ring and his papal banner.

At the consecration of a new abbey, William used the ceremony to proclaim an international crusade against the English. The knights who had initially refused to support him suddenly clamored to join. In the medieval world, all those who joined a crusade had their sins forgiven in advance, and some were even granted automatic passage into heaven. William had changed the prize to be gained from simple loot and plunder to the salvation of their souls. The invasion was on.

A Tale of Two Battles

On August 10, 1066, the Anglo-Saxon and Norman armies faced each other across the Channel and prepared for the imminent invasion, but it didn't come. The winds needed for the Normans to cross the Channel refused to blow and both armies were forced to wait impotently on their respective shores. This non-invasion had particularly dangerous implications for Harold. According to Anglo-Saxon law, the common men of the country were duty bound to serve in the King's army for two months of the year, and because of the delays, this time had already run out. With a deep sense of dread, on 8 September, with no other choice available to him, Harold disbanded his army.

The timing could not have been worse. No sooner had he done this, than he received catastrophic news. Tostig, his exiled little brother, had been busy in his absence and had returned, landing in Northumbria with 300 ships and 12,000 men led by his new best friend, the terrifying Hardrada, King of Norway, who also fancied himself as the new King of England. They marched through Northumbria unopposed, scattering the northern earls before them and seizing the town of York. But as they approached Stamford Bridge, just outside York, they had a nasty shock. There, waiting for them, was Harold and his army. Amazingly they had traveled 187 miles in four days, marching at breakneck speed from London to York, and in doing so had caught the Vikings completely by surprise.

The resulting battle was such a crushing defeat for the Norwegians that not only were both Tostig and Hardrada killed, but out of the original 300 ships, only twenty-four sailed back to Norway. The battle of Stamford Bridge was one of England's greatest victories and established Harold Godwinsson, at least in my mind, as one of her greatest heroes. It would have ranked alongside the defeat of the Spanish Armada, Trafalgar, or the battle of Britain, were it not for the dreaded news that greeted Harold as he paused to draw breath after his heroic victory.

William's fleet had landed near Hastings. As if crushing the Viking invaders were not enough, Harold was now going to have to fight the Normans. In an act of breathtaking fortitude, Harold gathered his battered and exhausted army, turned around, and raced back to London to fight his second battle within a fortnight.

The armies finally met on October 14, 1066. Before the onslaught, William added the final touches to his PR campaign. He planted his papal banner and even wore the holy relics upon which Harold had supposedly sworn around his neck for all to see. Then the two sides clashed in what was to be the longest battle in medieval history. It ground on for over eight hours, the Normans battering the defensive line of the Anglo-Saxons again and again as they stubbornly held the brow of the hill. As night approached, it looked as if all William's machinations would come to nothing as Harold's army still refused to yield. Then at last it was all over as the remnants of the Anglo-Saxons were showered with arrows and the courageous Harold famously met his end with an arrow in his eye. Around him lay over half the nobility of Anglo-Saxon England.

The Destruction of a Culture

If the battle of Hastings disrupted Anglo-Saxon society, the aftermath destroyed it. Like a modern-day presidential candidate, William had promised rewards to all those who backed him. Once victorious, the Norman nobles lined up to be given their share of the lands that had been conquered. What remained of the Anglo-Saxon nobility was dispossessed to make way for the new Norman overlords. The English did not take such injustice without a fight and an uprising erupted in the north. The suppression that followed resulted in mass genocide as William exerted his will over the whole country in a campaign of widespread murder and oppression. The invasion of England was to be complete, and the Normans made it clear that they had no desire to assimilate themselves into the culture of the land they had crushed, or to share their prize with anyone.

William's Unique Legacy

Despite his warlike credentials, William the Conqueror's most impressive legacy came in the form of the two unique works that he commissioned: The first in the realm of government, and the second in the world of art.

THE DOMESDAY BOOK

William was a master of manipulating perceptions and the interpretation of information, and so he knew how dangerous that talent could be. He knew how to talk his way into and out of anything, and he was determined not to let the inhabitants of England do the same to him, especially when it came to the taxes they owed him. To combat any attempts at tax evasion he developed the perfect weapon to prevent it, the Domesday Book, the world's first complete database.

The Domesday Book was a complete inventory of every property and possession in England and a record of who owned what. William used it to determine the exact amount of tax each person owed the crown. Its formidable title reflects his outstanding ability to communicate terror and obedience through metaphor. To the pious Christian inhabitants of England, "Domesday" had a resonant significance. The information the book contained was so accurate that its decisions were said to be as final as those of judgement day and the implications of disobedience the same. Death and taxes: Some things never change.

Through the Domesday Book William demonstrated his desire to control not only the land and the people of England, but also its information. This was the ultimate form of conquest. It is a tribute to his perception that he appreciated that although battles could win a country, only accurate information would allow him to control and manage it effectively.

THE BAYEUX TAPESTRY

The most famous and beautiful work of art that William commissioned is the 230 foot-long Bayeux Tapestry, created to tell the whole story (from William's point of view) from start to finish. Perhaps William felt insecure in his claim and needed to reaffirm it. Perhaps the PR guru in him wanted to make sure he, and not his detractors, had the final say. Through it, William demonstrated that he wanted to control not only the perceptions of his peers, but also the perceptions of posterity. It is the world's first press release, in the same way that the later tyrants of the twentieth century would produce promotional newsreels to justify their actions and claims. I wonder how different the tapestry would have looked if Harold had commissioned it, if he had been given the chance to tell his side of the story.

History is full of triumphalist art commissioned by the victors. But when I look past the beauty of the Bayeux Tapestry, I see a man trying very hard to convince me; perhaps too hard. It is as if he knew deep down that his launching of divine crusades and the legitimacy of his claim to the throne of England were more spin than substance, more opportunism than destiny, and it was this insecurity that compelled him to shout all the louder.

That is what makes the end of the tale all the more interesting.

William Comes Clean

William died aged sixty on September 9, 1087, while on campaign to secure some of his lands in France. On his deathbed, in a priory in Rouen, it was recorded that he made a frank and full confession. In it he admitted that he knew he did not have a real claim to the crown of England and that he had brutalized and robbed an entire nation. It was an incredible confession, but unfortunately we will never know if he actually made it. But whether he did or not, it reveals how his contemporaries saw him: As an amoral blatant opportunist. We can often tell how a person was viewed by their contemporaries by the way they are treated after their death. Harold Godwinsson's mutilated corpse was stolen away from Hastings and given a king's burial by his followers, who risked death to honor him. William the Conqueror's followers, however, all deserted him the minute he died, leaving his body lying naked and bloated on the floor of the church after his attendants had stripped it of anything of value.

SECTION TWO: LESSONS
THE MASTER OF MANIPULATION—WHAT WE CAN
LEARN FROM WILLIAM THE CONQUEROR

Until one is committed there is hesitancy, the chance to draw back, always ineffectiveness. Concerning all acts of initiative (and creation) there is one elementary truth, the ignorance of which kills countless ideas and splendid plans; that the moment one definitely commits oneself, then providence moves too. All sorts of things occur to help one that would not otherwise have occurred. A whole stream of events issues from the decision raising in one's favor all manner of unforeseen incidents and meetings and material assistance which no man could have dreamed would come his way. Whatever you can do or dream you can, begin it. Boldness has genius, power, and magic in it. Begin it now.

Johann Wolfgang von Goethe

If there is one attribute that every famous historical character I have studied shares, it is boldness. The amazing figures who shaped their world, the same world we inherited and live in today, will always be remembered for their sheer audacity and daring, characteristics which often caused those around them to gape in utter disbelief. The same is true today. In the lessons from Alexander the Great I talked about summoning the courage to jump at your chance when life presents it to you. William the Conqueror helps us to expand this concept further. In chapter two we analyzed what drove Alexander and Genghis Khan to overcome huge challenges. Alexander was driven by desire, Genghis Khan by desperation and fear, but both believed that they had a mandate from the heavens to conquer the world. Both were driven by demons and destiny. It was as if neither of them had a choice. As a result their actions were incredibly bold, but this behavior was almost a by-product of their belief in themselves.

William the Conqueror was different. Despite his public proclamations, he did not believe that it was his divine right or destiny to conquer England. He promoted the myth that he was launching a righteous crusade, but deep down he knew it was a cynical fiction. He was the ultimate opportunist and he knew it. That is why I choose him as an excellent example of the characteristics of boldness. William of Normandy teaches us the power of guts and raw ambition with no other justification than the desire to succeed. He teaches us to go for it. Unfortunately, he also teaches us the implications of this power, if driven by corrupt and ruthless motives.

Boldness

Boldness is faith in action. Boldness is when we take that leap out into the unknown, out into the public arena, present our idea or plan for public consumption, risking ridicule, failure, and all the other emotions that terrify most of us. These emotions can be so strong that they are like an emotional straitjacket, causing the inaction that kills a million dreams in their infancy. Boldness is the cure. Bold action causes two responses, one simple to explain, the other profound. The first thing that taking action tends to do is dispel fear. Like my sky-diving story in chapter one, I was terrified, but once

I'd jumped, I realized that it was not as bad as I thought it would be. Think back over your past to the things that you were scared to do, yet once you gathered your courage and took action they were never as bad as you thought. In many cases the thing you were scared of turned out to be great fun. If you had not forced yourself to do all the things that you were scared of, how stunted would your life be today? We can all grasp this concept easily, as we all have plenty of examples of it, but the second reward of boldness is more elusive. . . .

"Ask and ye shall receive, seek and ye shall find, knock and the door shall be opened unto thee." I am always wary of quoting from religious texts because, I do not want to sound as if I am preaching, (and most importantly, I am not conventionally religious). However, I have repeatedly seen through all the religious traditions I have studied, the recurring theme of boldness, courage, and commitment being rewarded. These religious quotes are mirrored by secular writers such as the German author Goethe (see the quote at the start of this chapter), and in other sayings like "Fortune favors the brave." What have our ancestors known about the rewards of boldness since the earliest civilizations? What have they all been trying to tell us?

When you have the courage to act, something—call it God, life, the universe, whatever you like—helps you. It is as if life is meeting you halfway. Show that you are serious enough to act and life will send you what you need and give you a helping hand. As the saying goes "God helps those who help themselves." Interestingly, and perhaps more disturbingly, one of the major lessons I have learned from history is that if you take vigorous action your motives do not always have to be good. The power that helps the pure of heart also helps the corrupt. Just look at William the Conqueror.

I cannot tell you the number of times that after working for months on a project and seeming to get nowhere, an unsollicited phone call has come out of nowhere and not only brought my goal to fruition, but given me more than I had asked for and could have dreamed of. The sensation of some huge force moving to arrange circumstances in order to help me has been so strong that I have been overwhelmed by gratitude and humility. It is literally as if my prayers have been answered and I stand in childlike awe before this force. I have stressed over and over that this book is not about trite motivational catchphrases and empty positive thinking. Life is frequently totally unfair and brutal, but the fact remains that most of the things that I have achieved in my life were not achieved by my efforts alone. The people I needed to meet, the things I needed to happen, the opportunities I wanted, occurred with such graceful timing that I can speak from personal experience of the power that Goethe and other writers have been talking about for millennia. In all the above instances, I was amazed at my apparent luck, but now I know that I had done my part by stepping boldly out into the unknown.

This irrational calling to act, to trust, and leap out into the unknown is very difficult for a lot of people, especially the logical and analytical types. In my arena of launching businesses, the people I know who are extremely logical and analytical to the detriment of their emotional intelligence tend to make terrible entrepreneurs. They need everything to make total sense before they can act, but the ability to take

calculated risks can rarely be justified rationally and analytic-
ally. The patterns of our destinies do not usually conform to
spreadsheets. They rarely, if ever, make sense.

If you have trouble trusting your instincts, let me ask you
a question. Where do you feel fear? The clenching sensation
in your guts or chest? We refer to courage as "guts" and we
talk about having a gut reaction. Even our word for courage
comes from the French word *coeur*, or "heart." When you
are terrified, when life is telling you that you are in danger,
you do not think it; you feel it. What does this tell you? That
your body thinks. Our minds are not contained in our heads
but rather our mind and intelligence flow and are contained
in every cell of our bodies. This is what we try to express in
the concept of intuition. It is our deepest form of
intelligence, and as we all know it is invariably right. If you
have a bad feeling about something, and you go ahead with
it despite that feeling, you usually end up regretting it. The
converse is equally true. If you have a good feeling about
something, then have the courage to trust it and have faith in
it. You may not realize it, but you will still have thought it
through. It is just that a deeper part of you has been doing
the thinking. Of course do the analysis, think it through
logically, but do not use that to hide from the simple fact that
to build a dream takes blind faith, trust and courage. You
quite simply have to follow your heart, have guts, step out
into your future and *be bold*. You will not be alone.

Be wary of allowing your thoughts to rob you of courage.
Of condemning you to become a "nearly" man who almost
got their act together but whose dreams never graduated
past good intentions. Only actions get results. You will never
build a powerful life and achieve your goals based on what

you intend to do. I rarely listen to what people say, I always look at what they do. Have you ever heard the saying, "What you do screams so loud I can't hear what you say"? Action is everything, and it is action that makes your life into what you dream. Bold action is a big, bright, clear statement of confidence, and confidence is magnetic. Confidence is compelling. People who can really make things happen are rare. A lot of people talk but very few can act, and that is why boldness draws people to you.

Now please do not mistake boldness for bravado. Bold actions do not need to be loud ones. They also do not need to be big, they just need to be big for you. That is what makes something bold: The fact that you had to summon the courage to do it. So no matter how small the act is, if you feel nervous and it is a big deal to you, show some guts and life will meet you halfway. And sometimes it gives you even more. That is how you grow. You take the first step, get used to the nerves, then take the next, but every time you want to grow and expand in your life the need to be bold will be there.

When you step out boldly and declare your audacious plan, the world will look at you and will want to know one thing. OK, you have taken action, but do you have the other magical ingredient that Goethe was talking about in the quote at the beginning of this section, do you have commitment?

Commitment

Boldness and commitment go hand in hand. Bold actions without commitment are flashes in the pan; commitment without bold action lacks impetus. That is why Goethe highlights them both. People can be so scared of failure, that their actions very often are lackluster and lack commitment. The world picks up on their uncertainty and is therefore more likely to resist their actions, which further compounds their doubt. Our whole lives are littered with the debris of a lack of commitment: exercise machines that lie under the bed, and abandoned language courses. Any idiot can get enthusiastic about a new project, but it takes commitment to carry on with something once the initial enthusiasm wears off. The reason that we rarely see this is because commitment requires that rare and precious attribute: character. The ability to keep going even when it is uncomfortable and we don't want to. Our culture has become so addicted to comfort that the fact that commitment is often uncomfortable has made many of us commitment-averse, choosing instead to take the path of least resistance. The hardships that we often face in achieving anything of worth force us to constantly ask ourselves, "Do I really want this?" Often it is the psychological challenges that are the worst, as deciding to keep going, even though success is not in sight, means that we have to deal with the fear of failure and rejection. Commitment is a psychological game that we play with ourselves, and we all know that without commitment to a goal we won't stand much chance of achieving it. Despite the fact that commitment is often perceived as being boring or uncomfortable, the gift that it contains is the refinement of our character and the strengthening of our resolve. It also contains a magical quality that is revealed by the act of boldness. However, there is another aspect of it that is not as well understood: the effect that our commitment has on other people, especially those we are competing with. Here is an example of what I mean.

Years ago I was in a rough part of Glasgow with a friend of mine who is a successful entrepreneur. He grew up there and as a result is very streetwise and understands the rules of the environment that he was brought up in. As we walked down the street we suddenly found ourselves surrounded by a gang. As they began the preliminary chat before attacking us, my friend looked the leader in the eye and said very calmly "OK, boys, if you want to fight, fine, but you better make sure that you kill me, because if you don't, I will not stop till I win. I know where you all live, so if you don't finish the job tonight, I will track down every last one of you." Of course his language was a bit more colorful than that, but the meaning was the same and the effect it had on them was fascinating. They literally stopped in their tracks. You could see the doubt flicking across their eyes. It wasn't fear, as they outnumbered us by about five to one and there was no doubt that they could have beaten us to a pulp. But he had stepped into their minds and had questioned exactly what attacking us meant to them. They had wanted to beat some guys up for entertainment but certainly not murder anybody. They had absolutely no motive to do that, and he had psychologically upped the stakes way beyond what they were willing to commit to. He had shown that he was willing to do what they were not and his absolute commitment made them think twice. Of course his gamble relied on him being convincing and them believing him.

As I walked away, trying to keep my voice and knees from shaking, I asked him if he had meant what he said. He burst out laughing and said, "Of course not, but they never knew that." In chapter one we talked about the power of peer pressure. The gang were my friend's childhood peers. Having grown up in that area he knew the rules and how the game was played. I did not, and as a result would have tried to reason with them, which would have been a big mistake.

The effect that a person's commitment and bold actions have on those around them is fascinating to watch. It plays on people's doubts and fears and makes them think that you know something they don't. Most importantly, your absolute commitment makes your competitor question theirs, and if it is not as strong as they perceive yours to be, they will very often back down. Notice I said "as they perceive yours to be." Think about it: How do they know how committed you are? It is purely an impression based on what you say, your behavior, and body language.

In every area of life a totally committed adversary always causes potential opponents to pause. If you know that they will do whatever it takes and sacrifice everything to keep their business, family, or whatever, then you have to be sure that you want it just as badly. I see the power of absolute commitment in business all the time—some multinational decides to throw money at a project that will put a small businessman out of business. They think it is a good idea but are not emotionally committed to it. To them it is nothing, but to him his business is everything he has and as a result he will fight harder and longer and be willing to make sacrifices that the employees of the multinational will not. To them it is just a job; to him it is his house, his family's security, and his life's work. It is amazing how often an underdog's commitment beats a large budget hands down. When I am studying a competitor I do not look at their budget; I look at their level of commitment first.

I love commitment testers. They separate those who believe from those who think they do, or even worse just say they do. They also save a lot of talk. Here's an example: while I was writing this book, a guy approached a business friend of mine and asked him to invest in his company. My friend invited me to sit in on the meeting so I could give him my opinion. The guy gave us all his chat on how serious, determined, and committed he was, and how he would do whatever it took to make it work. All he wanted was a small fortune in return for a percentage of shares in the company. During his impassioned plea he had let it slip that he had $9,000 in savings. When he had finished I said "You will be investing your savings in the business, won't you?" I have never seen anyone squirm so much in my life. My friend brought the meeting to a close to save his embarrassment and never did make the investment. The $9,000 was a tiny sum compared to what the man was asking for, and it would not have made a huge financial difference, but that was not the point. It was a test to see how serious he was. He was willing to risk my friend's money but not his own, so how much did he really believe in his company? It was all talk. If he had opened with "I have an idea I believe in and I have put all my savings into it, can you help me?" we would have known he was serious.

Commitment testers are extremely important if you are about to embark on something that is really important to you, and you want to make sure that those involved with you will give their all. If someone is asking you to risk everything but they themselves have nothing to lose, then be wary. But it is also very useful to test yourself by asking what you would be willing to stake on a goal or project. You do not need to do anything; just say to yourself "OK, I am going to give my all to pass this exam. If I don't I will give $200 to charity" then observe your reaction. If you feel, "Well, that's $200 down the drain!" then you will need to look at why you think you will not do what it takes to follow through. Is it because you don't think you are capable of it, or is it because deep down you can't really be bothered? None of us are superhuman, so if you really want to achieve something but you feel that your commitment might waver, then a good idea is to tell your best friend that if you give up you will give them $200! This can be great fun, as you know that every time they see you, they will ask how you are doing, and every time you feel like giving in you can picture them showing you all the great things they bought with your money. That's a bit of Genghis Khan motivation for you.

So if you are about to embark on a new project, reflect on why you want to do it and exactly what winning means to you. How committed are you? Even if you are totally committed emotionally, clarifying the reasons in your mind will reinforce and strengthen your commitment. A good idea is to write a list of your reasons and the deeper motivations behind them. A person with one very strong reason to fight will be committed, but someone with twenty will be unstoppable.

William the Conqueror was totally committed to following through on his claim to the throne of England. It was not a passing fancy that he was willing to give up on. He showed his commitment and determination by not giving up when at first nobody wanted to back him. He instinctively knew the importance of persistence.

If at First You Don't Succeed—
The Power of Persistence

You must try and try, and keep trying until you do. This is the ultimate test of your commitment, whether it be to a relationship, in sport, or in business. Often when I am chatting to people they say to me, "You know, I think I would quite like my own business." But when they say it their facial expression and body language look as if they have been asked if they want red wine or white and they don't really mind which. By that I mean they sound as if it is a matter of no real consequence to them. I never say it, but I know that they probably will never start a business, as although they like the idea of the rewards, they have absolutely no desire to go through the inevitable pain and hassle it involves. They lack the necessary commitment. The minute the problems and challenges came along, they would realize that it was not really worth the pain to them and they would walk away in exactly the same way that the gang did in the previous section. If you want to succeed in something that is worth doing, you really need to have a burning desire to do it. I once asked one of the most successful businessmen in Britain what he thought were the main criteria for building a successful business. He answered "The desire to do it has to be an all-consuming obsession. It may not make you successful in relationships, but you need it to succeed in business." Yes, an obsessive desire to achieve something will take its toll on the rest of your life, but he was talking about achieving business success on a massive scale. In any arena, the bigger the goal, the bigger the obsession, commitment, and sacrifice needed. His answer may sound a bit blunt and extreme, but the fact remains that you will never succeed in your career if you are out the door bang on 5:30. And you will never succeed if you lack the commitment to persist through challenges and setbacks. However, being committed and willing to go through pain for your desire is not enough. We have to be a bit more intelligent than that and constantly adapt and refine our actions to ensure they are taking us in the direction we want to go. Boldness and commitment without brains is often a recipe for disaster.

Here is a phrase that I always repeat to myself when I feel as if I am banging my head against a brick wall. It helps me to focus on taking the most effective action to help me achieve my goals: "One definition of insanity is to keep doing the same thing over and over but to expect it to produce different results." Many people in life yearn for greater financial security or for more fulfilling relationships, but despite the fact that their actions are not achieving their desired goal they struggle on, hoping that their circumstances will miraculously change. Persistence is an admirable and necessary quality, but unfortunately persistence alone is not enough. What is essential in order to achieve your goals is persistence with an accurate cognitive feedback loop. What I mean is that as we move towards our goal we constantly check our actions to see if they are effective and adapt them accordingly. This may seem obvious but it is surprising how many people rarely do this and end up slogging away for years without realizing they are moving in the wrong direction. I call this "the Charge of the Light Brigade syndrome." At the battle of Balaklava, during the Crimean war there was a famous cavalry charge that, despite the courage, commitment, and heroism of the soldiers, ended in a disastrous massacre. The Light Brigade had been commanded to attack Russian gun positions and raced off towards them. Tragically, they had been misinformed as to the location of their enemy and charged in the wrong direction only to be blown to pieces by the guns that were shooting at them from another direction. I find this story a very powerful metaphor for those who, despite wanting to do their best and giving it their all, are pouring all their energies into ineffective action. If you find that you have been working on a goal for ages and can't seem to make any headway, just make sure that you are not indulging in your own personal Charge of the Light Brigade. However, if after examining your actions, you are sure that what you are doing is right, then keep going, and eventually you will reap the rewards of your persistence and commitment.

I used William the Conqueror as an example of boldness because he was a duke who dared to take on a king. His commitment and persistence are illustrated in the way he refused to give up when at first nobody agreed to back him, but I could just as easily have used Hannibal, Genghis Khan or any of the other characters in the book to demonstrate these attributes. In the next lesson, however, William stands supreme as a real master in a skill that is modern yet timeless. If he was alive today, he would probably have his own mass media network as he knew that to lead the masses you must master the art of controlling perceptions.

Master the Art of Controlling Perceptions

When I started my career, my first jobs were always in sales. Sales jobs are massively underestimated in our culture, but I knew instinctively that everyone in life, whether they liked it or not, was a salesperson, and that sales is simply the art of communication and the ability to compel another person to take action. The world's greatest salespeople to me were historical giants like Jesus Christ, Muhammad and, unfortunately, Hitler. The first two communicated their messages with such power that they changed the heart and soul of mankind; the latter communicated his message with such misguided passion that he demonstrated man's ability to create hell on earth. Similar skills, opposite effect. As we will see as we discuss William the Conqueror's formidable powers of persuasion, the message communicated does not even have to be true in order to compel people to act. When I realized that sales was really the art of persuasion and human influence, I felt compelled to learn everything I possibly could about it and to treat it like an art and a science. The skills I learned enabled me to fulfill my career goals and eventually set up my own businesses. Someone who builds a business empire has learned to persuade more people to buy from them. This sounds simplistic, but they have simply learned persuasion skills on a larger scale.

One of the things I learned when I began to study the art of persuasion was that the statement "a good salesman can sell anything" is complete nonsense. If the idea isn't right and the market conditions are wrong then even the best will struggle. I also know from repeated experience that a bad salesman can make an absolute mess of selling an excellent product or idea. The reason is perfectly simple: they do not have the first clue about how to communicate their message in a way that others understand. They have not mastered the art of persuasion and so cannot compel others to act or change their behavior. I have seen people struggling beside others who overachieved, despite the fact that they are working as hard as each other. The difference between them is the way that they talked about what it is they are trying to sell. The same principle applies to everyone, regardless of what it is they do for a living. Their effectiveness in getting what they want in life is in direct proportion to their ability to communicate with the outside world. Whether it is being able to let the people around you know that you care for them, or being able to persuade someone to give you a job, the ability to communicate your needs and wants effectively will ultimately determine how fulfilling your life is. I once heard a quote that I have never forgotten: "everything you need and want is either owned or controlled by another human being. So you owe it to yourself to get good at asking for it." Perhaps there is the odd exception, like spiritual enlightenment, but for 99 percent of the things we want the statement is true. Whether you like it or not, at some point in your life you will have to stand eyeball to eyeball with another human being and ask them for something. Whether you get it or not is determined by how well you understand how to "sell" your idea.

OK, so let's look at some of the key components of successful persuasion. As modern as these concepts are, you will see that they are exactly what William the Conqueror did.

"Reframe" Your Message Until People Understand It

Have you ever seen those T-shirts with statements like "It's not a bald patch. It's a solar panel for a sex machine"? Or "I am not overweight, I am undersized"? Well, as lame as they are, they are actually employing a psychological technique called reframing. As the name suggests, it simply means putting a different frame around a concept. This can have an immediate effect on the way we perceive a person, idea, or event. As I write this book there is a very clever advertising campaign being promoted by various well-known consumer food brands. Having seen the rise in consumer consciousness about health issues, they have decided to highlight some facts about their products that nobody has ever thought about: that they are rich in anti-oxidants and therefore good for your heart. This has probably always been true, but they have decided to totally reframe how we think about their products. The history of ideas is full of people changing how they thought about things. Slavery used to be seen as good business practice until people campaigned to have it reframed as barbaric inhumanity. But in the wrong hands this form of persuasion is disastrous. William the Conqueror was a master of it. "It's not a selfishly motivated invasion, it's a religious crusade." Or, my personal favorite "I haven't just fallen flat on my face in front of my whole army, I have grabbed England with both hands." Genius. Here are some others he would have loved. It's not genocide, it's "ethnic cleansing"; it's not sacking your work force, it's "downsizing"; it's not killing your own soldiers, it's "friendly fire." The reason the invasion of 1066 is so significant is because it shows how powerful the tools of persuasion can be when one man uses them to motivate the masses in the direction he wants them to go in order to fulfill his personal ambitions.

Reframing is also a very important skill to learn when it comes to communicating with ourselves. Remember, in chapter one we discussed how we interpret what events in our lives mean to us. One way of changing how we feel about something is to simply change the frame we choose to put around it; for example "My business going bust is not a dismal failure. I have just completed an invaluable crash course in what not to do, and I won't make those mistakes twice." Now, reframing does not mean that you continue to feel terrible about something, but try to think positively about it while denying your pain. No, it means transforming how you perceive the situation and so completely and genuinely changing how you feel about it. Here is an example. Imagine that you were in bed trying to sleep and all of a sudden someone started throwing stones at your bedroom window. How would you react? You would be shocked, then angry. You jump up and run to your window and there in the street is a little boy throwing the stones. You try to wave but he is so busy gathering more stones to throw that he can't see you. How do you feel now? Even more angry and indignant. You get dressed and run downstairs and bolt out the front door. Now you are furious. You are just about to start shouting at him when he turns round and through his tears says "Sir, sir, please help me, we have been in a car crash and my mummy and sister are trapped in the car." *Now* how do you feel? Resourceful, helpful, compassionate? You grab your cell phone to call 999 as you run with him to the accident scene. Would you say to him "Give me a minute to calm down. I am still furious at you for throwing stones at my window"? You would not even think about it, as your negative emotions would have evaporated. That is the power of a reframe. Done properly, it totally changes how people perceive the message you are giving them, and transforms the way you perceive a personal circumstance that you have chosen to reframe.

If something in your life really bothers you, reframing it can change the way you feel. So if you genuinely believe that your idea is great but nobody is taking you up on it, try taking a step back and reframing how they perceive it. Done right, it can have dramatic results, as William the Conqueror demonstrated. But how do you know what frame to put around your idea? That depends on the next essential skill in the art of persuasion: the ability to see the world through your audience's eyes.

Step Inside Your Audience's Mind

People who are inexperienced in communication and persuasion tend to cram their minds full of why they think their idea is a good one and why they think people should like it. The minute they get in front of their target, they vomit their opinions all over them. The point that they are missing is one of the key concepts that we have been discussing throughout this book: that people can represent the same events, ideas, etc. very differently to themselves, and that we are all capable of valuing things differently. Had William the Conqueror persisted in ranting on about why he wanted to invade England and expected everyone else to come around to thinking it was a good idea, he would have remained William of Normandy and disappeared from history.

An excellent communicator endeavors to get inside the mind of the person they are trying to persuade. There are two main ways you can do this—one is to try to empathize with them and imagine what it is like to be them by looking at the world through their eyes. The second way is to simply ask them questions and draw out their deepest feelings and opinions of your plan or idea. Just stop talking about what you think and listen to them. Once you see how they view the world, then you can begin to frame your idea in a way that they will understand. I do not mean that you lie to or manipulate them, but rather you simply ascertain what is important to them. Here is a real-life example:

I was once dealing with a huge financial company and had a product that was perfect for them. I had convinced all the line managers and they saw the benefits and wanted to go ahead with it, but the director of the department I was dealing with just would not give it the go ahead. I met with him over and over again and explained all the advantages, but he kept avoiding committing to it. I felt like William saying the same things repeatedly to his knights but just not convincing them. Finally I stood back and imagined I was the director; he was near retirement age, whereas all his managers were in their late twenties and, unlike them, he had never embraced new technology, and it was a cutting-edge technology product I was offering. In my imagination I kept pretending I was him until it hit me. His reluctance was nothing to do with the money he would save or how good the product was. He was simply afraid of being made to feel stupid in front of his managers as he did not understand the technology. Once I understood, I totally changed direction and invited him along to a training session about how to use the new technology, along with some of his older peers. He realized that it was very simple, and I made sure that he knew details that his staff did not and suggested that he train them how to use it. I reframed the product in a way that meant it was no longer a threat that made him feel stupid, but a chance for him to demonstrate his grasp of new technology and actually appear knowledgeable. Had I kept banging on about the product's merits, he would have become more entrenched. Is there someone in your life that you just can't convince? Take time out and see it through their eyes. Maybe changing direction like William the Conqueror will open the door for you.

Use Compelling Imagery

Imagine you are trying to convince somebody to do something.

Now think of their mind as an iceberg. You can see the tip of it revealed through the comments they make, but the deeper and more important feelings are beneath the surface. If you don't get them to open up and reveal their true thoughts then they will remain submerged. It is those hidden parts of the iceberg that will rip the bottom out of your boat, sink your plans, and cause your idea to have a cold and watery death.

OK, I laid it on a bit thick but what did I just do there? I wanted to compel you to discover the hidden feelings of the person you were trying to convince. So rather than saying, "Because it's very important," I used an analogy with a more terrifying image, one that conjures up images of the *Titanic* and freezing to death. A bit extreme, perhaps, but if that image resonated with you, then it had the required effect.

Imagery, metaphor, and analogy are incredibly powerful communication and persuasion tools. Metaphor is the language of our emotions and our dreams. Our subconscious talks in pictures. That is why we dream in images. If you say to a keen gardener that not keeping their finances in order is like not watering their prize roses, then they will understand it better than if you rant on about losing interest on their savings. If somebody loves football, use football analogies; if they are always reading special forces books, use military examples. Of course, we have to be subtler than that, but by using effective comparisons and examples your message will become more relevant, significant, and richer. Metaphor and analogy are two of the most powerful means of communicating with another person and entering their world-view. They allow you to step inside their mind to understand the way they see themselves and the world. Once we do that, then we can talk to them in the language that they talk to themselves. The master of this form of com-munication was Jesus Christ, with his use of parables. Parables are simply metaphors, and Jesus used them brilliantly to communicate his message to the masses. Here are some examples of his genius.

Rather than lecturing people on why they should not waste their abilities, he used the image of hiding your light under a bush or burying your talents (ancient coins) in case you lost them. This story has become so widespread that our language took the word "talent" from the ancient form of coinage. Rather than advising his listeners not to mix with idiots or give their time to ungrateful people, he said "don't cast your pearls among the swine" or "don't throw your seeds on rocky ground." The first conjures up the images of precious stones lying in the mud amongst snorting pigs; the second an act of wasteful futility. Powerful images create powerful emotions and communicate your message in a profoundly moving way. If people understand that a new idea which they are unfamiliar with is like something they *are* familiar with, and preferably have strong feelings about, then they will grasp the message more easily. Remember, words are simply our attempt to represent images and capture the emotions and concepts that create the fabric of our lives. By using language rich in imagery, we go straight to the source.

No matter who you are or where you are in life, the ability to persuade and communicate your ideas to others is essential. So let's look at how William the Conqueror did it.

PHASE ONE

William exploits the fact that Harold Godwinsson has been unlucky enough to be handed over into his custody. However, he treats him like an honored guest and even makes him one of his knights. This is a great honor to bestow upon Harold but it disguises William's true intent. In one stroke of brilliance William makes Harold beholden to him. He makes Harold his man and therefore eliminates a potential rival. But William would not be a master of the art of controlling the perceptions of his peers if he had left it at that. In a pantomime trick he makes Harold inadvertently swear over holy relics. It is hard for our modern minds to grasp the significance of this. Remember, we discussed in chapter one how Alexander was motivated by the possibility of immortality. By tricking Harold, William places a massive deterrent in his mind to ever opposing him. By breaking his oath, Harold would very possibly feel that he was going to go to hell. Imagine you were about to sit an exam, and you believed that by passing it your soul would be damned for eternity. How motivated would you be to study? This is a perfect example of the power of fear in motivation to prevent us from doing something. Furthermore, once Harold seizes the crown, William promotes the myth throughout all of Christendom that those who support Harold are also damned to hell. This is the type of psychological warfare that would have made Genghis Khan proud and would sap the strength of any pious warrior in the medieval age. William created a psychological conflict in Harold: Pursue the important goal of achieving the crown of England and you will risk the eternal life of your soul. In chapter one we looked at how we must align our goals with our highest values. William turned this against Harold and through his devious use of PR changed the gravity and significance of Harold's actions to create the circumstances he wanted. He constructed the opinion that Harold was a damned liar in the minds of both his supporters and his enemies. Long before Harold Godwinsson fell in the battle of Hastings with an arrow in his eye, he had been a victim of character assassination through William the Conqueror's perfectly orchestrated PR campaign.

PHASE TWO

Despite his careful manipulations, William was enraged to discover that Harold was more of a man than he originally thought, and that he was thwarted in his ambition to become king. So he asks his nobles to follow him to England to help him win the crown. What is wrong with this appeal? His request is all to do with his own needs and ambitions and nothing to do with those of his nobles. They would not say it to his face, but you know that they are thinking, "William,

I don't give a damn that you have been made a fool of. I am not risking my life and everything else I have for your ego and dynastic ambitions."

PHASE THREE

Had William not understood the dynamics of persuasion and the essential components of motivation he would probably have turned up the pressure on his nobles in terms of bribes and threats. This would have made his key supporters more resentful, and possibly have precipitated a rebellion in his own Duchy of Normandy, making his ambition of invading England even more unattainable. William was far too cunning to bang his head against a wall like that. What he did next was an act of such shameless audacity and blatant spin-doctoring that it acts as both an invaluable insight into how to convey our goals effectively and a warning to be wary of those who would try that against us.

Picture William in his castle, sitting alone late at night, in front of a fire. Let's imagine his thought processes as he ponders his original failed bid.

"Mmm, how can I persuade my nobles to support me in my invasion of England? What is important to them? Money, power, and land, but I have tried that, and they still have not signed up. Why? It must be because they feel the risks of attacking England are greater than the potential benefits they will receive. Also, they know that if we fail their lands and fortunes in Normandy will be at risk. They would like more power but not at the expense of what they already have. The problem is that they are too comfortable. And they also think that my claim is spurious. I have to make the invasion appeal to a part of them that they regard as more important than their lands. What is that? They are all deeply religious and their immortal souls are more important than all their earthly possessions. They are also more loyal to the Pope than to me. So how can I tap into that passion and loyalty? How do I convince them that supporting me in the invasion will be of benefit to their souls? I've got it! I will switch tactics and persuade the Pope that Harold is an oath-breaker and an enemy of the Church. If my nobles will not come for money, then they will if it means automatic entry to heaven. Also, anyone who does not support me will be seen as being outside the Church and an enemy of the Pope. So now I have the carrot and the stick. Perfect. Now I just have to convince the Pope. How will I do that? Well, I will start by promising him more lands in England. That always appeals to him."

And it did.

William's tactics exemplify perfectly what we discussed in chapter one when we talked about clarifying our values and aspirations and aligning our everyday actions with them. When he changed the meaning of his invasion from personal greed to a holy crusade, he appealed to his followers' deepest needs and highest aspirations, and so motivated them to do exactly what they had previously been opposed to. In chapter one, we looked at how to motivate ourselves; here William reveals to us the secret of motivating other people.

If you want to motivate yourself, align your actions with your deepest needs and highest aspirations. If you want to motivate others, align their actions with their needs and aspirations.

It really is as simple as that. However, this brings the realization that the ability to motivate the masses has no bearing on the purity of your intentions. Both Gandhi and

Jesus Christ did exactly the same thing as William, but had very different motives. That is why we have to be on our guard as to what ideas we are buying from those who are constantly trying to influence us.

A Word of Warning

I was once asked by an interviewer if there was any advice I could give people who were looking to invest in a new business or buy into new technologies. My answer shocked them. I said that the first thing they should do before they parted with their life's savings was to read *The Emperor's New Clothes* by Hans Christian Andersen. Do you remember the story? Here's a brief recap. Two tailors arrive at the court of a stupid and vain emperor and tell him that they can make him a suit out of magic cloth that you can only see if you are of extremely high intelligence. Of course the cloth does not exist, but the first adviser that the emperor sends to check on their progress is too scared to admit that he can't see it, so when the devious tailors mime holding it in front of him and say "Isn't it beautiful?" he answers "Oh, yes, it's exquisite." He then tells everyone in court how beautiful the cloth is. The second adviser does the same, which compels everyone else to lie. Peer pressure kicks in and makes the whole court fall into line, as everyone is too scared to admit the truth in case they appear stupid. The story culminates with the emperor parading through the streets in the buff until a child screams, "Look! The Emperor has got no clothes on!" In an instant, his childlike honesty breaks the collective tyranny that the adults have inflicted upon themselves and the whole crowd erupts in laughter. Excellent.

Not only is this story one of the best examples of negative peer pressure, but it warns us to have the power to stand up for what we believe in and have the courage to say what we believe. Think about it. The Third Reich and Hitler's rule was based on this disturbing trait in human nature. People like Hitler, and, on a lesser scale, William the Conqueror, have been conning the masses since the dawn of time. Imagine if the knights in William's court had simply said, "Crusade against England? Yeah, right, William!" Maybe he would have remained on the other side of the Channel.

Now you may think that this phenomenon occurs only in fairy tales and despotic regimes, but I see it in large corporations all the time. Some new management-speak comes out and overnight all the managers are using it, trying desperately to appear as if their finger is on the pulse. I have seen companies waste millions because of collective hysteria as they stampede to invest in the next big thing, as they are terrified of missing out and so appearing stupid. It is essential that we have the courage to be like the child in *The Emperor's New Clothes* and bring clarity and honesty when the people around us, through fear of appearing uncool or stupid, are collectively deluding themselves.

That is why I urged you in chapter one to think about your values, who you are, what is important to you, what motivates you and why. If you know who you are and what you believe in, you are less susceptible to the manipulations of others and less likely to follow the herd. You will be able to spot when somebody is trying to exploit your fears to make you march in line and sign up for their master plan. But before you go spinning off the edge of the world ask yourself: how will history judge you?

How Will History Judge You?

Stop reading and ask yourself this question: If I were to succeed in achieving my most cherished goal, what would be the implications of my success?

This question makes us ask ourselves how pure our motives are and how much integrity our ethics have. Remember, despots and saints have used the same methods of communication, but for very different reasons. The reason that I stressed values so strongly in chapter one is because they are the guiding light or conscience of our ambition. Blind ambition is a hideous thing, as by its very nature it ignores the implications of its actions, believing always that the end justifies the means—a grotesque philosophy. William the Conqueror succeeded in conquering England and achieved his goal, but at what cost? He killed and brutalized an entire nation and suppressed the Anglo-Saxon culture. The fact that he did it under the guise of religious piety makes it all the more distasteful.

History is full of examples of characters "succeeding" but with horrendous consequences. Francisco Pizarro succeeded in conquering Peru and the Incas, but at what cost? The Incas had developed the world's first welfare state and had a rich, vibrant culture, all of which he completely destroyed because he wanted gold. "What does it profit a man if he gains the whole world but loses his soul?" We may be able to succeed by manipulating people's perceptions, but deep down we all yearn for truth and meaning. How empty would our lives be if all we had was spin and PR, with nothing real behind it?

Doing the right thing takes character, confidence, faith,

and courage, all the noble and beautiful human attributes. It also takes sage-like judgement, as the right thing is often open to debate. However, in most cases the difference between the right and wrong thing to do is obvious and our conscience will not let us ignore it. I have seen this repeatedly in business with people lying to win contracts or get the sale. Invariably those who indulge in this behavior lack the self-confidence and faith to believe that they can be honorable and still succeed. But doing the right thing is not simply a moral imperative; it also makes hard business sense and makes for a much easier life. I know many wealthy business-people who invest in new ventures. The other day I was chatting to an investor who was telling me why he had refused to invest in one business but had poured a lot of money into another one. His first comment was "I did not trust the directors of the first company, but the director of the second one was honest and I knew he was a man of his word." No matter how good your idea is, if you have developed a reputation for lacking honor and honesty, then you will find life increasingly difficult. People think that by being duplicitous they will get ahead, but they fail to realize that the world is tiny and word will get out. Staying true to your values takes courage, but people admire it and years later you will find that doors will be open to you that would have been slammed shut if you had betrayed these values. It is important that we do not succumb to the pressures of the moment and give in to destructive decisions and behavior.

The Last Word from the Last Hero

If you do feel this pressure, then take faith from the last Anglo-Saxon king and the true noble hero of the tale, Harold Godwinsson. Look at the bigger picture. To me, history is the ultimate big picture. Hindsight not only makes us wiser, but helps us see more clearly. Harold Godwinsson was seen at the time as being an abject failure, but despite William's desperate attempts to cover up the truth, when we study the story, Harold emerges as the most noble of all the protagonists—the courageous king who was outmanoeuvred not by courage but by devious dishonesty and cynical manipulation. He is a character we can take inspiration from. So if you are being lied about or being forced to compete with those who are less than ethical, take comfort from the fact that people are very perceptive in discovering liars. It may not happen overnight, but given enough time they are nearly always found out. Maintain your dignity, hold fast to your standards, and believe in who you are, because at the end of the day that is all you have. If you feel tempted to betray your conscience and values for short-term gain, stop and ask yourself "How will history judge me?"

The last character in this book epitomizes that spirit. A woman in a male-dominated world, she sought to conquer no one and had no vast armies to protect her. Vulnerable throughout her life to forces outside her control she survived through her courage, strength of character, and the clarity of her values. For this, she is the last and perhaps greatest hero in this book. It is time to meet Elizabeth I.

5

Elizabeth I

Section One: History

The King paced frantically up and down the corridor, tortured by the sounds of his Queen's labor pains coming from behind the door. The intrigues of the last few years raced through his mind: the break with Rome and relinquishing the Catholic faith; risking his immortal soul to divorce his first wife, Catherine of Aragon, leaving his first daughter Mary illegitimate and splitting England in two, Catholic against Protestant. He had been willing to risk all of this to make Anne Boleyn his new Queen. A queen who would give birth to a son and provide him at last with an heir to the throne of England. Suddenly he stopped mid-stride. The screams of a newborn child cut through the air. Henry VIII ran to the door to be met by an anxious courtier. "Sire, your Queen is well and has delivered a healthy child . . . a girl."

Elizabeth I was born on September 7, 1533. She was the

product of the most famous divorce in history. From the day she was born, everyone—including her parents—mourned the fact that she was not a boy, a future king for England. But if Henry had desired an heir with a courageous heart and character of steel, then his wish had been granted. Unfortunately for Anne Boleyn, a male child did not follow and as a result Henry ordered her execution on trumped up charges of adultery. Little Elizabeth would not only have to deal with her father's crushing disappointment at her gender, but also with the fact that the father she adored had murdered her mother.

Twenty years later, in 1553, things got a lot worse for the young Princess. Her half-sister Mary was crowned Queen and began taking revenge for the long years of humiliation that Henry's divorce of her mother had caused. Mary was a fanatical Catholic and used her power to attempt to force Catholicism back onto Protestant England. Her religious fanaticism resulted in over three hundred people being burned at the stake, their only crime being that they were Protestant. Mary also reinstated the marriage of her Spanish mother and disallowed Henry's marriage to Anne Boleyn. To her, Elizabeth was always "the little bastard," and her mother "the great whore."

Elizabeth's very existence had rendered Mary illegitimate and her mother a widow despite years of faithful marriage. To Mary, Elizabeth symbolized all the pain and humiliation she had endured. Furthermore, she was Protestant. Mary placed Elizabeth under immense pressure to give up her religion and marry a suitor of the Queen's choice. She accused her sister repeatedly of being a traitor, and Elizabeth came very close to meeting the same fate as her mother. She was threatened with disinheritance, imprisoned in the Tower of London, and held under house arrest for years. However in 1558, Mary I died, and the twenty-five-year-old Elizabeth was crowned Queen of England. She must have felt as if she had been delivered from the jaws of hell.

But her problems were far from over.

In Tudor England, the concept of an unmarried and childless queen was inconceivable, even grotesque. The reigns of Mary and Elizabeth were even referred to as "the monstrous regiment of women." The pressure on the new Queen to get married became unbearable; her advisors made it clear that she did not have a choice. Their strategy was to use Elizabeth to cement a strong ally in Europe; both France and Spain saw her as a useful pawn in their power politics. If she was vulnerable when her increasingly delusional half-sister was on the throne, as Queen of England, Elizabeth's exposure to danger was relentless, with invading armies, countless assassins and treacherous allies using every opportunity to end her reign.

Detested by Catholics at home and abroad, Elizabeth had far more enemies than friends; Scotland posed a constant threat of invasion from the north, and Scotland's traditional ally, France, from across the channel. In 1570, Elizabeth I was excommunicated by the Pope, who then instructed England's Catholics to rise up against her. By the end of her reign, Elizabeth had survived at least twenty assassination attempts. Furthermore, England's economy was in chaos, and English credit was so low that they had to pay 14 percent on all loans borrowed from the European money markets. No one expected her to last.

However, Elizabeth's most bitter adversary was King

Philip II of Spain, the most powerful monarch of the age. During his loveless marriage to Mary, he demanded Elizabeth's execution. After Mary's death, he shamelessly made Elizabeth an offer of marriage as a convenient means of extending the vast Spanish empire. According to Spanish courtiers, "the sun never set" on Philip's empire. (Sound familiar? This is precisely what was said of the Darius II's Persian empire in chapter one.) When Elizabeth refused Philip's proposal, the Spanish King realized that she could not be controlled by such traditional means and thus resorted to more direct methods.

Throughout her life, Elizabeth had been threatened and bullied, but now she was the about to face the greatest danger of all.

The Spanish Armada

On August 7, 1588, Philip II launched his Armada of 130 ships to escort 27,000 professional soldiers with the sole purpose of crushing England. His goals were clear; to stamp out Protestantism and prevent England from colonizing the New World. To ensure victory Philip invested a colossal $12,000,000 in the campaign. (At the time the total annual income of England was only $354,000!)

The situation appeared hopeless; Elizabeth only had 4,000 trained soldiers. The rest of her army was made up of terrified conscripts and undisciplined militias. Furthermore, they had virtually no ammunition and had already started deserting. It seemed as if nothing would stop the battle-hardened Spanish veterans when they landed. To make matters worse, Elizabeth was almost bankrupt and diplomatically isolated. She couldn't raise loans at home or abroad because Spain was the favorite to win. Philip, on the other hand, had been fending off wealthy European states wanting to invest in this invasion, and his diplomats had forged deals to ensure that England would receive nothing.

The story is the stuff of legends, and like all great legends it has a great hero, for as with all the other challenges in her life, Elizabeth would have to face it alone. With the Armada off the coast of England, she addressed her troops at Tilbury. To this day her words stir the blood.

> Let tyrants fear . . . I am come amongst you, as you see, resolved, in the midst and heat of the battle, to live or die amongst you all, to lay down for my God, and for my Kingdom, and for my people, my honour and my blood, even in the dust. I know I have the body of a weak and feeble woman, but I have the heart and stomach of a King, and a King of England too, and think foul scorn that Spain or any prince of Europe should dare to invade the borders of my realm . . .

Elizabeth had faced her fear and the fates were moved to intervene. The Royal Navy met the Armada in the English Channel and engaged in a furious sea battle. They managed to drive the Armada into the North Sea, where it was scattered in storms. Only a third of the fleet ever made it back to Spain.

The implications of Elizabeth's courage in the face of the Armada are vast. If they had landed then, not only would Britain be unrecognizable, but there would have been no

British empire and the United States of America would have evolved very differently.

Elizabeth went on to reign unmarried for another fifteen years, until her death on March 24, 1603. She left a legacy of unprecedented stability in England, and by the end of her reign it had emerged as a world power. The vulnerable young girl had become the greatest monarch England ever had.

SECTION TWO: LESSONS

The Unconquerable Self

I thank God that I am indeed endowed with such
qualities that if were turned out of the realm in my
petticoat, I were able to live in any place of
Christendom.

Elizabeth I

Elizabeth I is the perfect character to end with as her
vulnerability makes her the easiest to relate to, as well as the
most courageous of all the characters in this book. From
the day she was born she was cast into conflicts not of her
making and vulnerable to forces far greater than herself. She
had no armies to back her and no one to protect her. Yet she
faced the dangers alone and grew to become the mightiest
monarch England has ever had. Why was this? Historians tell
us that throughout her life, even during her darkest years,
there was one thing that she could always rely on: her
character. She knew deep down that no matter how bad
things got, she would always see herself through. And that is
the greatest lesson that Elizabeth I teaches us.

In the introduction to this book I talked about how we
all have resources within us that are capable of overcoming
the hardest challenges. Often we only really tap into this
power when we are tested beyond our limits. Some people
say that this is our true character, and that it cannot be
created or developed, only revealed when tested. Others
believe that character is built and honed by challenges in life.
However, I believe that character is a function of how we

view those challenges, what they mean to us, and our self-image. Strength of character can be learned. Despite the trials she faced, Elizabeth was blessed with this trait from an early age. She was her own rock and never faltered. But rather than being a rare gift that only the chosen few have, I believe we can all be like this if shown the tools.

So in the closing chapter of this book rather than simply talking about the power of character and a strong identity, I want to leave you with some tools that you will be able to apply immediately and so demonstrate for yourself that strength of character is not a gift but rather a way of seeing yourself and the world around you. The first of these was developed by the Italian psychiatrist Roberto Assagioli. He created the discipline of psychosynthesis and pioneered the use of creative visualization and imagery to facilitate personal growth. It is particularly powerful for creating a sense of your inner strength and ability to overcome challenges.

THE DIAMOND

Visualize a diamond in your mind's eye. See its perfection, its beauty. It has many sides, many facets, but it is one whole. The word "diamond" comes from the Greek word *adamas*, "unconquerable." It was transformed from a dull piece of coal into a diamond by the immense heat and pressure it endured. Its trials created its beauty. As you quietly mediate upon this diamond, understand that you are not your fears, your worries, you are not your job, your nationality, nor your habits. Your "self" is as perfect as the diamond. It is unconquerable, eternal. Let this image and its meaning flow through you and then, when you are ready to, take the image of the diamond and place it within your heart.

This very simple visualization instills in us a deep inner confidence and serenity that no matter how bad things get our true identity, our "self," remains unconquerable. We may be experiencing bad times but they are only experiences. Our true self cannot be harmed.

The diamond visualization has profound implications for our concept of who we are. This next one is a visualization that I developed for my little nieces as a game instead of reading them bedtime stories. It is more light-hearted, but just as powerful, and an excellent way of developing buoyant optimism.

THE CORK

The image of the cork is a powerful communicator of our ability to stay afloat no matter what life throws at us or how stormy it gets.

Close your eyes and imagine you are a cork bobbing about in the middle of the sea. The sea is calm, the sun is shining, and the sky is clear.

Now imagine clouds gathering and the sea becoming choppy. The skies darken and thunder roars as a storm breaks.

You are being tossed about in the waves, battered from side to side. Huge waves crash down, covering you. Make the storm as bad and the seas as rough as you can. Really experience the feelings of a horrific sea storm. But no matter how bad it gets, you keep bobbing back to the surface. You cannot sink no matter how perilous the conditions.

After a while, imagine the sea calming down and the sun coming out. The sun warms your face and there you are, a little cork bobbing away on the surface, unsinkable, able to weather any storm.

This may seem silly but let me give you a real life example of the effect it can have. A good friend of mine is very talented, but prone to bouts of despair if she suffers even the most minor of setbacks. Her emotions conspire to create a downward spiral that set off an emotional chain reaction and sends her plummeting. I taught her this little visualization and suggested she use it as she fell asleep each night. The results were fascinating. After only a couple of weeks she said that she had an enhanced sense of optimism and that when she suffered disappointments she just knew deep down that she would be OK. The words she used were "I may feel bad for a second but then I just bob back up." Those of us who are blessed with optimism or prone to despair are simply using imaginary and internal metaphors that either support or depress us. By using our imaginations, we take control of processes that were previously occurring beneath the surface of our souls.

Let's continue with the nautical theme and finish with an example that Elizabeth I may have related to.

THE LIGHTHOUSE

Imagine yourself on small ship in the middle of the ocean. It is pitch black, a storm is raging, and the ship is rolling from side to side. You are desperately trying to steer as the rain batters down on your face and the wind howls around you.

Experience this as vividly as you can. Feel the fatigue in your muscles, your fear as the realization sets in that you are totally lost and will soon succumb to the storm.

Suddenly in the distance you see a brilliant light piercing the darkness. It is a lighthouse. Now you know that all you have to do is follow its unwavering light and you will be safe. Feel the sense of security and relief that seeing the lighthouse brings. As you draw close, you can see the magnificence of its structure as it stands above the waves, solid upon the rocks. Now as you look up at it, feel yourself floating out of your body and becoming the lighthouse. Feel your unwavering strength and security. You are your own security, your own guide. You light the path to your future and are the rock upon which it will be built. You are all you need.

Do not underestimate the power of harnessing our imaginations. Einstein developed the theory of relativity by imagining himself riding on a beam of light into space. Many psychiatrists have proven that in a contest between will-power and imagination, our imaginations will always win. I have studied countless methods of curing phobias and trauma resolution; and telling a terrified person to "pull themself together" or "fight the fear" is a complete waste of time. Only by using the language of our emotions and dreams can we communicate with them. Our imagination is made up of pictures and sensations. When we sleep, we do not dream in words, we dream in pictures. They are the language of the soul.

Our Trials Teach Us Compassion

I stumble over the glacier like a drunkard, sweat pouring from me like spilled wine, a dying man clings to my back. I carry him through hell for what seems like forty days and forty nights, cherished images of my family and friends begin to flicker and fade to dull, lifeless fictions, as if that life had never existed. I realize that soon I too will collapse, and we will die together on a frozen wasteland, beneath an empty sky, far from home.

At that point I am catapulted from sleep, my heart and breath racing, my mind saturated in horrors. I sit in the darkness on the edge of my bed and rock back and forth praying that I will be given the strength to make a difference, and gradually I am allowed to return to sleep.

I went to Kashmir to climb a mountain, to add another notch to my belt. It was an egotistic desire, but life presented me with what I really needed, something deeper. I will never be able to dislodge the image of Sher's eyes when he saw my face after I came off the satellite phone and started to cry in sheer rage and frustration. As the tears froze to my face, he knew he was going to die, knew that I would leave him. Why would a rich westerner risk his life to save a poor Kashmiri tribesman? To this day, I am haunted by the image of those eyes, and I will never be able to close my heart to them.

When I returned home to Britain I was a different man. The spoiled middle class boy I had once been was left dead on the glacier. In the frozen wastes of K2 it is too cold for anything to live. There is only rock, ice, and death. I remember when I walked out, I finally descended to an altitude that could support plant life. It was near a village and I was assaulted by the smell of pine needles and little children laughing. I fell to my knees and drank in the sensations, consumed with gratitude as the little children danced giggling around the bedraggled madman. Returning to life after nearly losing mine made me feel that I had been given a second chance. Made me realize what we often take for granted. It transformed me. But the effect went beyond simple gratitude. I knew that in all our lives there were people who had been abandoned and were "dying," who needed help, but were screaming with silent voices. They are all around us, we see them everyday, but we are blind to it or choose not to see. All we have to do is reach out to them. Do one small thing to help them and carry them to safety. As I said in the story of the starfish in chapter three, you can't help everyone, but the ones you do help will never forget it. It can be as simple as having coffee with someone at work who is having a hard time. And by doing so, you will not only help them, but help yourself as well. In chapter two we talked of the transforming effect of terror. K2 was my "Scrooge experience." I saved Sher's life, but he also saved mine, so I like to think that he and I are even.

All my professional successes have been in emerging technologies, but my passion, my real interest, is in humanity. Technology has advanced at breathtaking speed, but humans have remained unchanged. That is why the lessons from the heroes of history are still relevant today. On the expedition I had more state of the art technology than a secret agent. I sent the message for help via e-mail and satellite phone, and it crossed the frozen wastelands in the blinking of an eye, but the message still came back, "cannot assist." We have the technology to send cries for help across the world at the speed of light, but it could take a millennia for it to travel the last few inches and reach our hearts. All the technological advances in the world are pointless if we lose our compassion and humanity.

The reason I admire Elizabeth I is because her trials taught her compassion. She knew what it was like to suffer from religious persecution, to be imprisoned, and threatened with execution. She had seen the horrors of the burnings that her fanatical half-sister had used to try to drag protestant England back to Catholicism, and as a result, she never subjected English catholics to persecution. Quite simply she knew what it was like.

Our personal trials teach us compassion. Without it we are no better than brutes. Compassion makes us human.

Compassion is easier to feel when we understand that we are all muddling through life, trying to do the best we can, with the limited knowledge we have. We may be adults but, emotionally, many of us are still terrified children living in fear of life, the future, and demons of our own making. Many of us still live in fear of the monsters under our beds, we just call them different names now. You may chastise yourself and others for their stupidity, but if you knew a better way you would do it. Of course we may know that we are being selfish, cruel, or petty, but unless that knowledge leads to a change in our behavior then we do not really "know" it. As I said in chapter two, "to know and not to do, is not to know." Even if a person is being cruel, grasping, or manipulative, it is often because only by hurting others can they make themselves feel secure. Deep down they are only trying to protect themselves, albeit in a very counter-productive manner. This realization helps us become more compassionate towards other people's failings and towards our own.

Elizabeth's response to the long years of vulnerability and uncertainty she experienced as a teenager and into her early twenties also demonstrates another important lesson. In chapter two we looked at how the same motivation to act can have very different outcomes, depending on what options you have. While Genghis Khan's childhood pain motivated him to use his power to destroy anyone who threatened to betray him, Elizabeth's response to her insecure childhood was to become wise and compassionate.

Of course they were both from different worlds, but pain feels the same no matter who or where you are. Her example teaches us to be on our guard as to the effect our experiences have on us. We have all seen people who have endured trials in their lives and as a result have become gentle and compassionate, whilst others have become jaded and bitter; their behavior becoming overly aggressive and harsh. This observation is the underlying theme of this book. Will we buckle under the challenges of life or face them heroically, using them to grow and become larger than life and so go on to ease the burdens of others? The choice is yours, but when you are struggling through the hard times, remember that you are doing the best you can and treat yourself compassionately.

The Art of Personal Reinvention

> Lord, we know what we are, but know not what we may be.
>> William Shakespeare, *Hamlet,* Act IV, Scene V

Throughout the ages and across cultures there is a recurring theme in the most significant stories that we tell one another: personal transformation. This concept resonates at a very deep level in all of us, whether it be as momentous as the story of Christ rising from the dead after three days or as innocent as the ugly duckling emerging as a beautiful swan. We all know instinctively that an essential feature in overcoming challenges in our lives will be our personal transformation; from fear to courage, enslavement to liberation.

Elizabeth I is a wonderful example of this process. She transformed herself from a vulnerable princess to an invincible monarch. I wonder how she felt in her later years when she looked back at paintings of herself as a young girl. To remember all the things she had to face and overcome. Elizabeth once said, "If I was then who I am now, no one could have hurt me." Did she wish the strong woman she had become could have protected the vulnerable girl in the picture?

Despite the dramatic transformations of characters in literature, in real life, transformation tends to creep up on us unnoticed. Here's a personal example. When I was writing this book, I bumped into two people in a coffee shop that I had known from my first job six years ago. We chatted about how things were in the industry and as they talked, I was amazed to see that they were still going through the same small problems, and doing the same things as when I worked there. They hadn't changed. Once they had finished they said "So what have you been up to?" I didn't know where to start and so just said "Umm, you know, this and that."

As I left, I was amazed at just how much I had accomplished and I realized that I was a completely different person from the one they had known. If money is a symbol of achievement, I now earn more as a guest business speaker talking for forty-five minutes than I earned in two months there, and I only do talks for fun. I do not mean to be crass and imply that money is a symbol of a person's worth; but to demonstrate that if, six years ago someone had shown me my future, the things I would achieve, the people I would have the privilege of working with, I would not have believed them. The reason that meeting was so significant to me was because at that time I was feeling pretty exhausted. I was writing this book through the night, and running two fast-growing companies during the day. As I had been standing in line in the coffee shop, I had been mentally berating myself for not doing more and working more efficiently. But when seen in context I realized just how far I had come.

The reason I'm telling you this story is because now that you have read this book, I hope that I have encouraged you to start your own quest, to find your own heroes, and begin to realize what you are capable of. It is at the start of your journey that you are most vulnerable to discouragement. Once you start pushing yourself you will sometimes feel as if you are getting nowhere, as if it is all struggle and no reward. It can sometimes feel that we are not making any difference at all to our lives but what we do not see is the internal transformation that we are undergoing. The changes that are taking place internally. It is only when we look back that we can see just how much we have changed and how small the problems are that used to bother us. We gain perspective and can finally appreciate our success.

In chapter one, I asked you to think about your dreams and your deepest desires. Often when we gaze up at that bright golden future, it seems to us that we are a million miles from it, and that we will never be able to achieve it or become the person it demands of us. In chapter four we discussed the power of metaphor in our lives. Here is one of mine: pursuing a challenging goal is like climbing a mountain. You stand at the bottom and gaze up, wondering how on earth you will ever get to the top. As you climb, you go through every emotion and physical state: determination, excitement, enthusiasm, boredom, drudgery, fear, rage, elation, fulfillment, and triumph.

Sometimes your route is blocked and you have to change direction, but if you keep going you will get to the top. One step at a time. And not only is the view from the top amazing, but with every step you take, the view gets better. I always remember that when I am experiencing tough times pioneering my new businesses. That metaphor is very real to me, and as a result, it helps me to understand and frame the experiences of my everyday life.

But unlike climbing a mountain, when we set out on our journey we never really arrive. The challenges never go away, they're just always a little bigger than we are, constantly forcing us to grow. The irony is that when we look back at our trials, we are often very grateful to them once we see the transformation that we have undergone. As we saw in chapter three, "Life has to be lived forwards but it can only be understood backwards."

The pursuit of a treasured dream can completely transform us and the greatest gift we receive is the inner transformation that occurs. The person we will be once we achieve our goal is not the person we are now. This realization reveals the true gift contained in the pursuit of a worthy goal:

It is not what you get, it is who you become.

Notice I said the pursuit of the dream and not the fulfillment. The fulfillment of a dream is a wonderful thing, but life does not always work out the way we want it to. We may fall short of the destination that we envisaged, but often the journey is so magical and exciting that once we embark on it, we find friendships and rewards along the way that we never expected. "Aim for the moon because even if you miss you'll still be in the stars."

The Courage to Become

What lies behind us and what lies before us are but tiny matters, compared to what lies within us.

Ralph Waldo Emerson

As I write this closing chapter, I have a card on my desk inspired by the Japanese philosophy of Zen that reminds me of the young Elizabeth I. It is a simple depiction of "courage." When most of us imagine scenes of courage we see sword-wielding warriors leaping into battle or other images of daring and heroism. Zen sees it differently. With its illuminating wisdom, it portrays courage as a tiny frail flower straining through the rocks, striving to reach the sun. Despite its vulnerability, it has had the courage to try. If it had been content to stay as a seed, its shell would have kept it safe for decades. But by keeping the world out, it would also have kept itself in. By striving to fulfill its destiny, it risked the dangers and pushed out into the unknown. In Zen the image of the seed battling to push through the rocks and soil, and having the blind faith that there will be enough water and light to ensure it's survival, is a powerful representation of the trials we will also have to overcome in order to break through the "shell" of our old self-image, and discover who we really are, and what we are capable of. We are like the flower, facing the same fears and unknown dangers of this world alone; armed only with our courage, our faith and the vision of what we were intended to be.

Of course you feel safe in your shell, you can stay in the same job, country, relationship. But at what cost? You will never know what strength of character lay dormant within you, what wonders were waiting to be revealed. But most importantly, as I mentioned at the start of this book, a life without risk is a dangerous illusion. Run from life and it tends to chase you. Hide from it and it comes looking. But look your fears in the eye and they tend to blink first.

Life is not safe. There is no security. Ultimately the only thing you can have faith in, is yourself. You are the only constant reality in your life. The rest is just window dressing. Wherever you go, there you are. Let me write that again. Wherever you go, there *you* are. Some people spend their whole lives running from themselves; changing careers, lovers, and cars, anything to try to change the external realities of their life, when what they really yearn for is the strength of character to face it. They fail to realize that their external reality is simply a reflection of their internal one and so they look to other people and their environment to prop themselves up, in the mistaken belief that they can be pro-tected from life; wrapped-up cosily in a security blanket.

Careers and status may come and go, friends and family and lovers will die. All you have is who you are; all you have is your character. And even the fickle twists and turns of fate lose their nameless terrors when we cultivate that deep inner conviction that no matter what happens in life, we will be able to handle it. We will always be there for ourselves. The world we take for granted today was built by "heroes"; countless, nameless, unsung heroes. Men and women of character who dared to believe and risk, sacrifice and endeavor. We are their inheritors. Now it is our turn. What will you do with the torch that has been passed on to you? What will you do with this gift? Learn from the countless heroes of the past to build the future you dream of. The life you long to lead will only be achieved by drawing on the heroic aspects of yourself: your courage, compassion, daring, determination, and all the other emotions that make us noble.

Our lives are a function of our character, and our character is a function of our courage. Never fear failure, never fear making mistakes. Fear doing nothing. Banish cynicism, pettiness, apathy, and all the excuses of the timid from your soul and commit to living to the highest aspirations of your heart. No matter how small you feel your life may be, determine to live it. . . . Heroically.

> The credit belongs to the man who is actually in the arena, whose face is marred by dust and sweat and blood; who strives valiantly; who errs and comes short again and again . . . who knows the great enthusiasms, the great devotions; who spends himself in a worthy cause; who at best knows in the end the triumph of high achievement, and who at the worst, if he fails, at least fails while daring greatly, so that his place shall never be with those cold and timid souls who know neither victory nor defeat.
>
> *Theodore Roosevelt,* Citizenship in a Republic,
> *April 23, 1910*

Bibliography

Alexander the Great

Arrian *Alexander the Great: Selections from Arrian (Translations from Greek and Roman Authors)*, Lloyd, J. Gordon (Translator) Cambridge University Press, 1981

Baynham, Elizabeth *Alexander the Great: The Unique History of Quintus Curtius*, University of Michigan Press, 1999

Bosworth, A. B. *From Arrian to Alexander: Studies in Historical Interpretation*, Clarendon Press, 1988

Fildes, Alan & Fletcher, Joann *Alexander the Great: Son of the Gods*, Getty Trust Publishing, 2002

Fox, Robin Lane *Alexander the Great*, Penguin, 1994

Grabsky, Phil & Chandler, David G. *The Great Commanders*, Pan Macmillan, 1995

Hanson, Victor Davis *The Wars of the Ancient Greeks and their Invention of Western Military Culture (The History of Warfare)*, Sterling Publishing, 1999

GENGHIS KHAN

Hartog, Leo de *Genghis Khan: Conqueror of the World*, Tauris Parke, 2004

Hoang, Michael *Genghis Khan*, Ingrid Cranfield (Translator), Saqi Books, 1990

Humphrey, Caroline & Onon, Urgunge *Shamans and Elders: Experience, Knowledge, and Power Among the Daur Mongols (Oxford Studies in Social and Cultural Anthropology)*, Oxford University Press, 1996

Kahn, Paul *The Secret History of the Mongols*, Cleaves, Francis Woodman (Translator), Cheng & Tsui Company, 1999

Liddel-Hart, Basil H. *Great Captains Unveiled: From Genghis Khan to General Wolfe*, Presidio Press, 1990

Polo, Marco *Travels of Marco Polo*, Viking Press, Latham, Robert (translator), 1958

Ratchnevsky, Paul *Genghis Khan: His Life and Legacy*, Thomas Nivison Haining (Translator), Blackwell Publishers, 1991

Spuler, Bertold *History of the Mongols: Based on Eastern and Western Accounts of the Thirteenth and Fourteenth Centuries (Islamic World Series)*, Fromm International 1989

Weincek, Henry, Lowry, Glenn D., & Heller, Amanda *Storm Across Asia: Genghis Khan and the Mongols: the Mogul Expansion*, Cassell, 1980

HANNIBAL

Bagnall, Nigel *The Punic Wars: Rome, Carthage and the Struggle for the Mediterranean*, Pimlico, 1999

Goldsworthy, Adrian *The Fall of Carthage: The Punic Wars 265–146 B.C.*, Cassell Military, 2003

Healy, Mark & Wise, Terrence *Hannibal's War with Rome: His Armies and Campaigns 216 B.C.*, Osprey, 1999

Livy, Titus Livius et al *The War with Hannibal: Books XXI-XXX of "The History of Rome from Its Foundation,"* Aubrey De Selincourt (Translator), Viking Press, 1965

Livy, B. R. *Hannibal's Crossing of the Alps*, Aubrey De Selincourt (Translator) Penguin Books, 1964

Prevas, John *Hannibal Crosses the Alps: The Enigma Re-examined*, Spellmount Publishers, 1998

WILLIAM THE CONQUEROR

Brown, R. Allen *William the Conqueror and the Battle of Hastings*, Pitkin, 1990

Douglas, David *William the Conqueror: The Norman Impact Upon England*, Methuen, University of California Press, 1967

Stenton, Sir F. M. *William the Conqueror and the Rule of the Normans*, F Cass, 1967

ELIZABETH I

Elizabeth I, Mueller, Jane. (Editor) & Marcus, Leah S.

(**Editor**) *Elizabeth I: Autograph Compositions and Foreign Language Originals*, University of Chicago Press, 2003

Elizabeth I, Pringle, Roger (Editor) *Portrait of Elizabeth I in the Words of the Queen and Her Contemporaries*, Barnes and Noble, 1980

Hibbert, Christopher *The Virgin Queen: Elizabeth I, Genius of the Golden Age*, Addison-Wesley, 1992

McLaren, A. N. *Political Culture in the Reign of Elizabeth I: Queen and Commonwealth 1558–1585*, Cambridge University Press, 1999

Thomas, Jane R. *Behind the Mask: The Life of Queen Elizabeth I*, Houghton Mifflin, 1998

Waldman, Milton *Queen Elizabeth I*, Collins, 1966

PSYCHOLOGY

Andreas, Steve & Faulkner, Charles *NLP: The New Technology of Achievement*, Quill, 1996

Bandler, Richard & Grinder, John *Frogs into Princes: Neurolinguistic Programming*, Eden Grove Editions, 1990

Dilts, Robert *Changing Belief Systems with NLP*, Meta Publications, 1990

Ferrucci, Pierro *What We May Be*, HarperCollins, 1993

Freud, Sigmund, Strachey, James (Editor) *The Complete Psychological Works of Sigmund Freud: "Totem and Taboo" and Other Works*, Vintage, 2001

Jung, Carl Gustav *Modern Man in Search of a Soul*, Routledge Classics, 2001

Jung, Carl Gustav *On the Nature of the Psyche*, Routledge Classics, 2001

Maltz, Maxwell *Psycho-Cybernetics*, Simon & Schuster, 1994

Meier, Carl Alfred *Psychology of C.G. Jung: The Unconscious in Its Empirical Manifestations*, Eugene Rolfe, (Translator), Sigo, P. 1986

Twight, Mark F. & Martin, James *Extreme Alpinism: Climbing Light, Fast and High*, Mountaineers Books, 1999